Promoting Wellness

for

Prostate Cancer Patients

Second Edition

MARK A. MOYAD, MD, MPH

*This book is dedicated to my dad and doctor,
Robert Moyad. He taught me what it means to put
patients first and what it means to be a good
husband and father.*

*It is also dedicated to my outstanding role models
and mentors—Dr. Bloom, Dr. Montie, and Dr. Pienta—
who helped create the environment that allowed
me to do things differently.*

*And finally, this book is dedicated to the individuals—
Epstein, Jenkins, Pokempner, and Thompson—who
invest in the dream and allow me to make a difference
one starfish at a time.*

All inquiries should be addressed to:
Ann Arbor Media Group, LLC, 2500 S. State Street, Ann Arbor, MI 48104
www.annarbormediagroup.com
877-722-2264

Printed in the United States of America

Ann Arbor Media Group Edition ISBN: 978-1-58726-565-5

Abbott Edition ISBN: 978-1-58726-567-9

10 9 8 7 6 5 4 3 2 1

CONTENTS

Learn from Probability

WELCOME to the SECOND EDITION of a unique educational book for individuals dealing with the many aspects of prostate cancer—from prevention to treatment and managing the common (and not so common) side effects of conventional therapy. This book has become one of the most widely distributed prostate cancer books in the world and has already been translated into multiple languages.

The goal of this second edition is the same as the first—to empower you with information and lifestyle suggestions to assist you in communicating with your doctor and other health-care professionals while dealing with this disease.

First and foremost, we thought it would be appropriate to consider potential lifestyle changes that you could adopt to help prevent heart or cardiovascular disease and potentially improve prostate health. You see, we live our lives based on probability. As you'll notice from the table below, cardiovascular disease is the number one killer of men, with cancer deaths ranking number two. If we can learn from probability and improve our cardiovascular health, we can reduce the leading health risk for men. The good news is that a heart-healthy lifestyle is one that is touted to also help prevent all the other common leading causes of death. By reducing your probability of heart disease, you will also reduce your risk of other diseases and early death. In chapter one, we will consider how to prevent cardiovascular disease.

Top Six Causes of Death for Men
1. Cardiovascular disease
2. Cancer (lung, prostate, colon, and others)
3. Accidents
4. Respiratory/Lung disease
5. Diabetes
6. Pneumonia/Flu

Next, we'll cover some of the nutritional and dietary supplements that you might take or avoid. This information should give you a starting point for discussions with your health-care provider regarding which of the supplements might be good choices for your personal situation.

The last three chapters of this book contain prostate-specific information. These chapters are intended to provide a quick "bottom line" review of everything from diagnosis, grading and staging, to treatment, including possible options for reducing side effects. This overview is not intended to replace more detailed sources of information or other books, but rather to give you the tools to make the most of your visit with your health-care professional. As promised in the earlier edition, we listened to you and your suggestions. We added additional information on treating side effects and included an expanded lifestyle and treatment section.

Finally, this book is dedicated to you—the individual dealing with this disease—and those around you who care for you and support you. You always have and always will be an inspiration. We hope that we meet your expectations with this latest edition and we continue to hope that one day soon, with more ongoing research and funding, this book will no longer be needed by anyone!

Mark A. Moyad, MD, MPH
Jenkins/Pokempner Director of
Preventive & Alternative Medicine
University of Michigan Medical Center
Department of Urology
Ann Arbor, Michigan
Email: moyad@umich.edu

CHAPTER 1

Heart Healthy Equals Prostate Healthy

As you'll remember from the introduction, cardiovascular disease (CVD) is the number one cause of death in men. Let me repeat this important fact—CVD is the number one cause of death in men—and that includes men diagnosed and treated with prostate cancer! Prostate cancer treatments are so successful today that after most men are treated, their risk of dying of prostate cancer becomes somewhat similar to the average man's without prostate cancer. So, what is the point of being treated for prostate cancer and not working to reduce your risk of heart disease? In addition, there is now plenty of clinical research to suggest that being heart healthy after being diagnosed with prostate cancer may actually increase the chances of beating prostate cancer itself! Therefore, in this chapter we will look at some ways that you can reduce your risk of developing heart disease and possibly improve prostate health as well.

MONITOR YOUR CHOLESTEROL AND BLOOD PRESSURE

Since the goal is not just to beat prostate cancer but to live longer and better, a man should know his cholesterol and blood pressure numbers as well as knowing the results of his latest PSA or prostate exam. A bonus to having your cholesterol measured is that it is a good indicator of how well your lifestyle changes are working. For example, in recent dietary studies of individuals with prostate cancer, it should not be surprising to learn that the individuals who followed the healthiest lifestyle programs also had some of the largest reductions in cholesterol.

So, let's explore what a cholesterol test involves. The blood test is usually done after fasting for 9 to 12 hours and measures four things—total cholesterol, LDL (bad cholesterol), HDL (good cholesterol), and triglycerides. Those items are worth some definition to help you understand their importance.

Total Cholesterol: an overview number developed with a formula applied to LDL, HDL, and triglyceride components. Lower numbers are better unless your HDL is really high.

Low-Density Lipoproteins: LDL, also called "bad" cholesterol, can cause buildup of plaque on the walls of arteries. The more LDL there is in the blood, the greater the risk of heart disease.

High-Density Lipoproteins: HDL, also called "good" cholesterol, helps the body get rid of bad cholesterol in the blood. The higher the level of HDL cholesterol, the better. If your levels of HDL are low, your risk of heart disease increases.

Triglycerides: Triglycerides are a type of fat that is carried in the blood. Lower numbers are better.

Cholesterol numbers are measured in mg/dL (milligrams per deciliter) in the United States and mmol/L (millimoles per liter) in other countries. The following table provides information on understanding your cholesterol scores.

TOTAL CHOLESTEROL	
Less than 160 mg/dL (Less than 4.14 mmol/L)	Optimal
160–200 mg/dL (4.14–5.16 mmol/L)	Desirable
201–239 mg/dL (5.17–6.19 mmol/L)	Borderline high
240 mg/dL or higher (6.20 mmol/L or higher)	High
LDL ("BAD CHOLESTEROL")	
Less than 100 mg/dL (Less than 2.59 mmol/L)	Optimal
100–129 mg/dL (2.59–3.34 mmol/L)	Near optimal
130–159 mg/dL (3.37–4.12 mmol/L)	Borderline high
160–189 mg/dL (4.14–4.90 mmol/L)	High
190 mg/dL or higher (4.92 mmol/L or higher)	Very high
HDL ("GOOD CHOLESTEROL")	
60 mg/dL or higher (1.55 mmol/L or higher)	Optimal
40–59 mg/dL (1.04–1.53 mmol/L)	Normal
Less than 40 mg/dL (Less than 1.04 mmol/L)	Too low
TRIGLYCERIDES	
Less than 150 mg/dL (Less than 1.69 mmol/L)	Normal
150–199 mg/dL (1.70–2.25 mmol/L)	Borderline high
200–499 mg/dL (2.26–5.64 mmol/L)	High
500 mg/dL or higher (5.65 mmol/L or higher)	Very high

Cholesterol testing is one of the best ways to predict the risk of heart disease. However, it may surprise you to know that almost 50 percent of the men and women who have their first heart attack actually have "normal" cholesterol numbers! This means that cholesterol testing is not perfect, just like the PSA test. However, also like PSA, it is the best blood test routinely available.

There are other blood tests that may improve the evaluation of CVD risk. The blood test that probably has the greatest chance of identifying those patients at higher risk of heart disease despite a normal cholesterol level is called "hs-CRP." This blood test should be requested and done at the same time that you get a cholesterol blood test. It measures low levels of inflammation that may be occurring, especially in the blood supply around or near the heart. It should not be done if you are feeling sick the day of the test or have a bad case of arthritis because that could falsely increase the number. Do not confuse this test with a basic CRP test (without the letters "hs" in front of it), because the basic CRP test is not as sensitive for predicting heart disease. The good news is that many lifestyle changes (good diet, exercise, weight loss) and medications (aspirin, cholesterol-lowering drugs) that reduce cholesterol can also reduce the hs-CRP number.

HIGH-SENSITIVITY C-REACTIVE PROTEIN (HS-CRP) RESULT	WHAT DOES THIS MEAN?
Less than 1 mg/L	Low risk (ideal)
1–3 mg /L	Moderate risk
Greater than 3 mg/L	High risk

In addition to knowing your cholesterol numbers, you should have your blood pressure checked regularly.

BLOOD PRESSURE (SYSTOLIC/DIASTOLIC)	WHAT DOES THIS MEAN?
Less than 120/80 mmHg	Normal = low risk.
120–139/80–89 mmHg	Pre-hypertensive (moderately high or pre-high blood pressure) = moderate risk.
140/90 mmHg or greater	Hypertensive (high blood pressure) = high risk.

It may be a good idea to purchase your own automated blood pressure reading machine for use at home. Your local pharmacist can guide you to a reliable machine that is inexpensive. Since many people experience "white coat hypertension" (falsely elevated blood pressure in a doctor's office), regular checks will give you a much better gauge of your blood pressure than having it checked once or twice a year in the doctor's office. I strongly recommend that everyone buy their own blood pressure device and monitor their blood pressure at least several times a month.

Your Goal Get your cholesterol and hs-CRP measured annually (or more often as needed) and discuss your results with your doctor at the same time as you discuss the results of your prostate cancer tests—one is not necessarily more important than the other. Monitor your blood pressure regularly. Use the cholesterol and blood pressure goals listed in the previous tables as a guide for discussions with your health-care professional.

MAINTAIN A HEALTHY WEIGHT

It seems that maintaining a healthy weight may be one of the most important things individuals can do not only to reduce the risk of cancer, but also the progression of the disease. Weight is generally measured in a clinical setting by measuring your body mass index (BMI), waist circumference (WC), or waist-to-hip ratio (WHR).

The BMI chart that follows is a quick way to assess your situation, but it does come with one major catch. An individual who has a lot of muscle mass may have a falsely high BMI.

This is why the WHR should also be considered. To calculate your WHR, measure your waist circumference (WC) at your navel and your hip circumference at the widest point (over buttocks). Divide your waist circumference measurement by your hip measurement. A high number is a concern. The WHR is a good measurement of abdominal or belly size. Discuss these results with your doctor.

WAIST CIRCUMFERENCE (WC) FOR MEN
35 to 39 inches (89–100 cm) = overweight
40 inches (101 + cm) or more = obese

BODY MASS INDEX AND RISKS OF OVERWEIGHT

WEIGHT (lb) → · HEIGHT (ft/in) ↓ · More risk / Less risk

HEIGHT	120	130	140	150	160	170	180	190	200	210	220	230	240	250	260	270	280	290	300	310	320	330
4'5"	30	33	35	38	40	43	45	48	50	53	55	58	60	63	65	68	70	73	75	78	80	83
4'6"	29	31	34	36	39	41	43	46	48	51	53	56	58	60	63	65	68	70	72	75	77	80
4'7"	28	30	33	35	37	40	42	44	47	49	51	54	56	58	61	63	65	68	70	72	75	77
4'8"	27	29	31	34	36	38	40	43	45	47	49	52	54	56	58	61	63	65	67	70	72	74
4'9"	26	28	30	33	35	37	39	41	43	46	48	50	52	54	56	59	61	63	65	67	69	72
4'10"	25	27	29	31	33	36	38	40	42	44	46	48	50	52	54	57	59	61	63	65	67	69
4'11"	24	26	28	30	32	34	36	38	40	42	45	47	49	51	53	55	57	59	61	63	65	67
5'0"	23	25	27	29	31	33	35	37	39	41	43	45	47	49	51	53	55	57	59	61	63	65
5'1"	23	25	26	28	30	32	34	36	38	40	42	44	45	47	49	51	53	55	57	59	61	62
5'2"	22	24	26	27	29	31	33	35	37	38	40	42	44	46	48	49	51	53	55	57	59	60
5'3"	21	23	25	27	28	30	32	34	35	37	39	41	43	44	46	48	50	51	53	55	57	59
5'4"	21	22	24	26	28	29	31	33	34	36	38	40	41	43	45	46	48	50	52	53	55	57
5'5"	20	22	23	25	27	28	30	32	33	35	37	38	40	42	43	45	47	48	50	52	53	55
5'6"	19	21	23	24	26	27	29	31	32	34	36	37	39	40	42	44	45	47	48	50	52	53
5'7"	19	20	22	24	25	27	28	30	31	33	35	36	38	39	41	42	44	45	47	49	50	52
5'8"	18	20	21	23	24	26	27	29	30	32	34	35	37	38	40	41	43	44	46	47	49	50
5'9"	18	19	21	22	24	25	27	28	30	31	33	34	35	37	38	40	41	43	44	46	47	49
5'10"	17	19	20	22	23	24	26	27	29	30	32	33	34	36	37	39	40	42	43	45	46	47
5'11"	17	18	20	21	22	24	25	27	28	29	31	32	34	35	36	38	39	41	42	43	45	46
6'0"	16	18	19	20	22	23	24	26	27	29	30	31	33	34	35	37	38	39	41	42	43	45
6'1"	16	17	18	20	21	22	24	25	26	28	29	30	32	33	34	36	37	38	40	41	42	44
6'2"	15	17	18	19	21	22	23	24	26	27	28	30	31	32	33	35	36	37	39	40	41	42
6'3"	15	16	18	19	20	21	23	24	25	26	28	29	30	31	33	34	35	36	38	39	40	41
6'4"	15	16	17	18	20	21	22	23	24	26	27	28	29	30	32	33	34	35	37	38	39	40
6'5"	14	15	17	18	19	20	21	23	24	25	26	27	29	30	31	32	33	34	36	37	38	39
6'6"	14	15	16	17	19	20	21	22	23	24	25	27	28	29	30	31	32	34	35	36	37	38
6'7"	14	15	16	17	18	19	20	21	23	24	25	26	27	28	29	30	32	33	34	35	36	37
6'8"	13	14	15	17	18	19	20	21	22	23	24	25	26	28	29	30	31	32	33	34	35	36
6'9"	13	14	15	16	17	18	19	20	21	23	24	25	26	27	28	29	30	31	32	33	34	35
6'10"	13	14	15	16	17	18	19	20	21	22	23	24	25	26	27	28	29	30	31	32	34	35

BMI < 25 = Healthy weight
BMI 25–29 = Overweight
BMI ≥ 30 = Obese

$$BMI = \frac{lbs.}{inches^2} \times 704$$

$$or = \frac{Kg}{m^2} \left(\frac{\text{weight in kilograms}}{\text{height in meters}^2} \right)$$

11

WAIST-TO-HIP RATIO (WHR)	HEALTH RISK
Less than 0.9	Low risk
0.9–1.0	Moderate risk
Greater than 1.0	High risk

I'm sure that you are wondering what is the problem with having a large waist. The real fat problem in humans is visceral fat (found deep around the liver, intestines, and stomach) as compared to subcutaneous fat (found just under your skin). Deep belly fat or visceral fat can cause lots of problems, whereas subcutaneous fat is not necessarily as unhealthy as it is unsightly and unattractive to some people. If you lose an inch or more of visceral fat, your cholesterol and blood pressure will generally drop almost immediately—a 2-for-1 bonus!

Your Goal *Have your BMI, WC, and WHR measured by your doctor and recorded in your medical chart. The goal is to maintain a normal BMI, WC, and WHR, or work to reduce your weight so that these numbers move toward a normal range.*

EXERCISE AND MOVE MORE—INCLUDING WEIGHT LIFTING

What if I told you that you could take a magical pill and reduce your risk of developing some of the most serious health conditions listed below. Would you take it?

HEALTH CONDITION	REDUCTION IN RISK OF OCCURRENCE OR PROGRESSION OF THE DISEASE
Alzheimer's disease & some other types of dementia	30–40%
Colon cancer	30–50%
Depression	25–50%
Erectile dysfunction (ED)	25–50%
Heart disease (& all types of CVD)	40–50%
Osteoporosis	40–50%
Premature death (sudden death)	30–50%
Prostate cancer, prostatitis, prostate enlargement	25–50%

Sure you would! Suppose I told you that the magical pill was 30 minutes of exercise (your choice of activity) every day? Are you surprised to find that there are so many beneficial results of exercising?

Exercise comes in a variety of forms and you should pick the one that works for you long term. Some people like to walk or climb stairs; others like to swim, row, or use a treadmill or elliptical machine; and others still like to garden. Basically, the amount of physical activity you should do and the frequency of the activity are dependent on your weight. An individual should do enough exercise to help himself maintain a healthy weight. Obviously though, the more active you are the better.

Exercise intensity is often measured using a metabolic equivalent task (MET) score. A single MET is the energy that is expended by just sitting quietly. MET scores are used by some researchers to calculate the average intensity of a specific exercise. MET scores for specific exercises are defined as the ratio of the metabolic rate associated with a specific activity divided by the resting metabolic rate. For example, if someone walks at an average pace, they are generally assigned a MET score of 3; jogging, a MET score of 7; and running, a MET score of 12. The higher the number of METs during your exercise routine, the greater the workout for your heart. You will see this principle in action the next time you get on an exercise machine that reports METs.

Also, keep in mind that weight lifting is probably as important as regular aerobic exercise. Weight lifting lowers your risk of osteoporosis, lowers your risk of type II diabetes, helps you to maintain a healthy weight, reduces the risk of heart disease, increases energy levels, and may improve your quality of life.

The following table gives you an idea of weight-lifting exercises that might be included in an exercise routine. Talk with your doctor to see which of these exercises might be appropriate for you.

WEIGHT-LIFTING EXERCISE	INITIAL REPETITION	ADDITIONAL REPETITION
Biceps curl	12 to 15	8 to 10
Chest press	12 to 15	8 to 10
Latissimus pull-down	12 to 15	8 to 10
Modified curl-ups	12 to 15	8 to 10
Overhead press	12 to 15	8 to 10
Triceps extension	12 to 15	8 to 10
Calf raises	12 to 15	8 to 10
Leg curl	12 to 15	8 to 10
Leg extension	12 to 15	8 to 10
Spine bone building exercise*	8 to 12 modified push-ups	8 to 12 modified push-ups

*Some doctors or trainers also like to include a back lift in order to strengthen the spine. A small weight (just a few pounds or kilograms) is placed on the upper back between the shoulder blades. While lying on your stomach, do 8 to 12 modified push-ups (stomach stays on the floor, hands clasped together behind your head, and lift your upper body up then down, up and down). This places resistance on the spine and may improve bone mineral density in this area.

Your Goal Take your exercise pill every day! Pick exercises that you enjoy. The amount of time you exercise should depend on your weight—whatever it takes to maintain a healthy weight is best. Begin to give weight lifting the same importance as aerobic exercise.

WORRY MOST ABOUT THE CALORIES—NOT JUST FAT

Research in the past has focused on lowering your overall fat intake in order to maintain a healthy body. Recently this has been challenged (thank goodness!). Controversy over this issue probably now exists because it is rather easy today to consume an excess of total calories from fat, protein, or sugar due to changes in portion sizes. In the past, most calories came largely from fat. The old saying "everything in moderation" means that lowering your caloric intake along with regular moderate exercise seems to make the most sense!

To show you what I mean about changing portion size, look at the table relating soda portion sizes and calorie content. This increase in portion size in the United States is also seen in every-thing from burgers to desserts.

DECADE	SERVING SIZE	TOTAL CALORIES
1960s	8 ounces	100
1970s	12 ounces	150
1980s	16 ounces	200
1990s	20 ounces	250
2000s	24 ounces	300

Not surprisingly, the average weight of children ages 12 to 17 has also increased with the portion sizes.

GENDER	1960s	2000s
Boys	125 pounds (57 kilograms)	141 pounds (64 kilograms)
Girls	118 pounds (54 kilograms)	130 pounds (59 kilograms)

Again, total calories are the concern and not just fat, protein, or sugar. Consuming smaller portion sizes is the first step toward controlling calories.

After first considering your overall calorie count, you should consider the types of fat you are consuming. The following table gives you an overview of common dietary fats and their effects on your body.

TYPE OF DIETARY FAT	WHERE IS IT COMMONLY FOUND?	GOOD OR BAD FAT & IMPACT ON CHOLESTEROL
Monounsaturated fat	Healthy plant-based cooking oils (canola, olive), nuts	Good Lowers LDL & increases HDL
Polyunsaturated fat (includes omega-3 fatty acids)	Healthy plant-based cooking oils (canola, safflower, soybean), flaxseed, fish, nuts, soybeans	Good Lowers LDL & increases HDL
Saturated fat (also known as hydrogenated fat)	Non-lean meat, high-fat dairy, some fast foods	Some are bad Increases LDL & increases HDL (note how it increases HDL ... interesting, isn't it?)
Trans fat (also known as partially hydrogenated fat)	Some margarine, fast foods, snack foods, deep-fried foods	Bad Increases LDL & lowers HDL

There are two types of fat that you should be concerned about—saturated fat, also known as "hydrogenated fat," and trans fat, also known as "partially hydrogenated fat." High intake of these types of fat has been linked to heart disease and cancer. A comparison of the saturated fat and calorie content in different types of milk below shows how making a careful choice can reduce your saturated fat and, more importantly, calorie intake.

TYPE OF MILK	SATURATED FAT IN A SERVING (8 OUNCES)	TOTAL CALORIES IN A SERVING (8 OUNCES)
Soy milk	0 grams	80–100
Skim milk	0 grams	80
1% milk	1.5 grams	100
2% milk	3 grams	120
Whole milk	5 grams	150

Choosing some of the more healthy fats, such as monounsaturated and polyunsaturated fats, is not only heart healthy, but also seems prostate healthy. A recent study showed that men consuming lower amounts of saturated fats and calories also had a lower risk of prostate cancer returning after treatment.

Your Goal *Make calories your concern, not just fat, protein, or sugar. Consuming smaller portion sizes is the first step toward controlling calories. Good fat and protein sources may also reduce* *your appetite and increase your HDL. If you are concerned about fat intake, choose items that are low in saturated and trans fat, and increase your intake of monounsaturated and polyunsaturated fat.*

NUTRITION LABELS

Do you know how to read a nutrition label? Are the following cholesterol-lowering margarine and sandwich healthy products?

NUTRITION FACTS SERVING SIZE = 1 TBSP.	
Calories 70	Cholest. 0 mg
Fat Calories 70	Sodium 110 mg
Total Fat 8 g	Total Carb. 0 g
Sat. Fat 1 g	Protein 0 g
Trans Fat 0 g	
Polyunsat. Fat 2 g	
Monounsat. Fat 4.5 g	

Healthy product low in calories, high in healthy types of fat (poly- and monounsaturated) and low in the unhealthy types of fat (saturated and trans fat). It is also low in cholesterol, sodium, carbohydrates, and protein, which is why it is also low in calories.

NUTRITION FACTS SERVING SIZE = 1 SANDWICH (208g)	
Calories 760	Cholest. 165 mg
Fat Calories 430	Sodium 1450 mg
Total Fat 48 g	Total Carb. 38 g
Sat. Fat 20 g	Protein Not listed
Trans Fat Not listed	
Polyunsat. Fat Not listed	
Monounsat. Fat Not listed	

Unhealthy product—it is high in calories and high in the unhealthy types of fat (saturated and probably trans fat). It is also high in cholesterol, sodium, carbohydrates, and probably protein, which is why it is also high in calories.

***Your Goal** Read nutrition labels and request the nutrition information at restaurants as a good way to control calories and decide what is truly healthy and unhealthy for you. Talk to your health–care professional or a nutritionist for more information on how to read nutrition labels.*

DIVERSIFY YOUR INTAKE OF FRUITS AND VEGETABLES

Eat a variety of fruits and vegetables and not just tomatoes, pomegranates, or whatever other specific fruit or vegetable du jour is getting all of the commercial attention currently. And never be impressed by the antioxidant amount or value of a fruit or vegetable. All fruits and vegetables, regardless of their color, have something to offer or their own unique healthy components that need to be appreciated. All fruits and vegetables have some research to suggest they have anti-cancer and, more importantly, anti–heart disease properties.

Be careful to limit fruit and vegetable juices and especially the exotic fruit drinks! You want more antioxidants, but many of these juices are high in calories and price. Some of the so-called healthiest juices are actually unhealthy unless consumed in moderation (less than 8 ounces a day) because they contain too many calories, and they can ultimately contribute to making you obese and unhealthy. Notice from the table below how most fruit and exotic juices have as many or more calories than a cola or beer.

Beverage Calories

BEVERAGE	APPROXIMATE CALORIES (8 OZ. SERVING)
Mixed fruit smoothie	200–250
Acai juice	150–200
Grape juice	170–180
Pomegranate juice	140–160
Pineapple juice or cherry juice	130–150
Orange, grapefruit, or apple juices or lemonade	100–120
Beer/wine/hard liquor	100–150
Watermelon juice	100–110
Cola and other soft drinks	100
Skim or soy milk	80–100
Carrot juice	70–80
Cranberry juice	70–80
Light beer	70–80
Blueberry juice	50–60
Sports drink	50
Tomato juice or mixed vegetable tomato-based juice	50
Coffee (with fat-free milk to cream)	5–50
Tea (black, green, Oolong)	5
Diet soft drink	0
Water	0

CONSUME MORE OMEGA-3 FATTY ACIDS

Omega-3 fatty acids, especially from fish, are not only heart healthy but, you guessed it, they are also prostate healthy. One of the largest medical studies of fish consumption found that eating fish several times a week was associated with a lower risk of advanced or aggressive prostate cancer. Some recent research suggests a lower risk of cancer recurrence after conventional treatment when fish intake was increased.

However, there has been a recent concern that some large fish (king mackerel, shark, swordfish, and tilefish) contain high concentrations of mercury, which can be bad for your health. This concern is generally important for women who are pregnant or trying to get pregnant and young children.

Both wild fish and farmed fish are good sources of omega-3. Farmed fish are fed products that contain fish protein and fish oil. Wild fish actually have a slightly more unpredictable amount of omega-3 because the amount depends on the maturity of the fish and when it is caught. It should be kept in mind that the positives still outweigh the negatives for farmed fish. In other words, the amount of contaminants in farmed fish is usually low, and it is still better to eat these fish than to not eat fish at all. Eating commercially prepared fried fish (restaurants, fast food, frozen) should be discouraged or minimized as it provides no health benefit, is low in omega-3, and high in trans fat.

Recent studies of farm-raised fish (such as salmon) have shown that they can contain as much as 50 to 75 percent less vitamin D compared to wild fish. Some farm-raised salmon also have vitamin D2, whereas the more natural vitamin D3 is found in wild salmon. The cause of this difference requires further investigation, but farm-raised fish is still considered healthy to eat.

The following table gives the approximate omega-3 oil concentrations from a group of fish and shellfish and shows how many servings a week would be required to give you the government–recommended daily intake (250 to 500 mg/day or 1,750 to 3,500 mg/week) to protect your heart.

19

FISH/SHELLFISH*	OMEGA-3 TOTAL AMOUNT (EPA + DHA) IN 1 SERVING (APPROXIMATE)	SERVINGS/WEEK TO MEET TOTAL OMEGA-3 RECOMMENDED DAILY ALLOWANCE
Anchovy*	1,165 mg	2
Catfish (farmed)	250 mg	7
Catfish (wild)	350 mg	5
Clams	240 mg	7
Cod (Atlantic)	285 mg	7
Cod (Pacific)	435 mg	4
Crab (Alaskan king)	350 mg	5
Fish sandwich (fast food)	335 mg	5
Fish sticks (frozen)	195 mg	9
Flounder/Sole	500 mg	4
Halibut	740 mg	3 (high in mercury)
Haddock	200 mg	9
Herring* (Atlantic or Pacific)	1,710 mg	3
King mackerel	620 mg	3 (high in mercury)
Lobster	70 mg	25
Mackerel (Atlantic)*	1,060 mg	2
Mahimahi	220 mg	8
Mussels	665 mg	3
Oysters (Eastern, farmed, Pacific)	585 mg	3
Pollock (Alaskan)	280 mg	7
Salmon (farmed)*	4,500 mg	Less than 1
Salmon (wild)*	1,775 mg	1 (high in vitamin D3)
Sardines*	555 mg	3
Scallops	310 mg	6
Shrimp	265 mg	7
Shark	585 mg	3 (high in mercury)
Snapper*	545 mg	3
Swordfish	870 mg	2 (high in mercury)
Tilapia	100-150 mg	20
Tilefish or golden bass	1,360 mg	2 (high in mercury)
Trout* (rainbow, farmed, or wild)	580-800 mg	3
Tuna (fresh)	900 mg	2 (moderate to high in mercury)
Tuna (light, skipjack)	230 mg	8
Tuna (white, albacore)	735 mg	3 (high in mercury)

*Fish in bold are moderate, practical, and generally safe to eat to get your recommended daily allowance of fish oil for heart health. It's okay to deviate several times a month, like eating halibut or regular tuna, because they are high in omega-3.

Your Goal *Eat several servings of fish per week. Baked, broiled, and even raw fish (sushi) can be healthy, but try to avoid fried fish.*

CONSUME MORE PLANT ESTROGEN FROM SOY AND FLAXSEED

The so-called plant estrogens are found in high concentrations in soy and flaxseed products. (This form of estrogen should not be confused with prescription estrogen that is many, many times greater in dosage.) Both of these products are heart healthy and may reduce your cholesterol. In addition, they are low in saturated and trans fat, high in fiber, and just overall prostate healthy. The Food and Drug Administration (FDA) suggests that 25 grams a day of soy protein from a variety of traditional sources may reduce the risk of heart disease along with a reduction in saturated fat intake.

The following table reviews some of the healthiest and cheapest traditional soy products according to plant estrogen and protein content that also contain little or no saturated or trans fat.

SOY PRODUCT	1 SERVING	TOTAL PLANT ESTROGEN LEVEL
Soybean	1/2 cup	175–200 mg
Tempeh	4 ounces	60 mg
Soy protein powder	1/3 cup	45 mg
Tofu	4 ounces	40 mg
Soy milk	1 cup	20 mg
Soy sauce	10 gallons	0

Like soy products, flaxseed can be a great tasting and healthy addition to your diet. Whole or ground flaxseed may be purchased in the vitamin/supplement department of most retailers carrying these types of products. You can grind the whole seeds or purchase containers of ground flaxseed. Although golden flaxseed is usually a little more expensive, it contains more fiber. So if you want to increase your fiber intake, golden flaxseed is a good choice. However, you cannot go wrong with either form of flaxseed. Like most foods that are high in fiber, too much (more than a few tablespoons a day) can be upsetting to your system.

Your Goal *Make soy and flaxseed a part of your regular diet.*

LOOK FOR HEALTHY COOKING OILS

Cooking oils that are high in monounsaturated fat, high in natural vitamin E, high in omega-3 fatty acids, and lower in saturated and trans fat are not only heart healthy but also seem to be prostate healthy. Oils such as soybean, canola, olive, and safflower are just some of the healthy oils out there. Do not just focus on olive oil, because numerous oils are beneficial. However, be careful of the amount used because 1 tablespoon of any oil contains approximately 120 calories (everything in moderation)!

Your Goal *Utilize a variety of heart-healthy oils in moderation. Read nutritional labels to make sure your oil is high in monounsaturated and polyunsaturated fats and low in saturated fats.*

GOING NUTS IS GOOD FOR YOU!

Most nuts are high in vitamins such as vitamin E, high in other antioxidants, low in saturated fat, high in monounsaturated fat, and some even contain omega-3 fatty acids. Also, nuts as a snack give you a sense of being full without getting too many calories. It is interesting that nuts such as walnuts, almonds, pistachios, Brazil nuts, and others have been associated with a lower risk of sudden cardiac death, and they contain compounds associated with prostate health. For example, Brazil nuts are one of the largest natural sources of selenium, and other nuts are some of the largest natural sources of vitamin E.

SOME NUTS AND SEEDS (SERVING = 1 OUNCE OR 1/4 CUP = 150–200 CALORIES)	NUTRITION
Almonds (170 calories)	High in monounsaturated fat (10 g) Polyunsaturated fat (4 g) Saturated fat (1 g) High in potassium (210 mg), fiber (3 g), and vitamin E
Brazil nuts (190 calories)	Monounsaturated fat (7 g) Polyunsaturated fat (21 g) Saturated fat (4 g) High in potassium (190 mg) High in selenium (6–8 times the recommended daily allowance)
Cashews (160 calories)	High in monounsaturated fat (8 g) Potassium (160 mg)
Chestnuts (50–100 calories per 3 roasted nuts)	Equal amounts of monounsaturated (0.1 g), polyunsaturated (0.1 g), and saturated fat (0.1 g) Lowest in calories and fat, and high in water content High in potassium (600 mg) and fiber (1.5 g) Only nut with a lot of vitamin C (about 10 mg)
Hazelnuts/filberts (180 calories)	High in monounsaturated fat (13 g) High in potassium (210 mg) and fiber (3 g)
Macadamia (200 calories)	Monounsaturated fat (17 g) Polyunsaturated fat (0 g)
Peanuts (170 calories)	Higher in monounsaturated (7 g) compared to polyunsaturated fat (4 g) High in potassium (190 mg) High in resveratrol (anti-aging compound?)
Pecans (200 calories)	High in monounsaturated fat (12 g) High in fiber (3 g)
Pine nuts (190 calories)	High in polyunsaturated fat (10g) High in potassium (170 mg)
Pistachios (160 calories)	High in monounsaturated fat (7 g) High in potassium (300 mg) and fiber (3 g)

continued next page

SOME NUTS AND SEEDS (SERVING = 1 OUNCE OR 1/4 CUP = 150–200 CALORIES)	NUTRITION
Sesame seeds (200 calories)	Almost equal amounts of monounsaturated and polyunsaturated fats High in healthy plant estrogen High in calcium (350 mg), iron (5 mg), magnesium (125 mg), potassium (170 mg), and fiber (4 g)
Soy nuts (150 calories)	High in polyunsaturated fat (2 times more) compared to monounsaturated fat High in potassium (325 mg) and fiber (4 g)
Sunflower seeds (170 calories)	High in polyunsaturated fat (9g) High in potassium (240 mg) and fiber (3 g)
Walnuts (190 calories)	High in omega-3 polyunsaturated fat (13 g) Highest nut source of plant omega-3 (ALA)

Your Goal Consume a variety of nuts to increase your intake of healthy nutrients and to help control your intake of calories.

CONSUME MORE FIBER—BOTH SOLUBLE AND INSOLUBLE

Many foods contain a high amount of fiber—beans, fruits, vegetables, bran cereals, flaxseed, whole grains, and oats, to name a few. These products not only lower cholesterol but they also seem to reduce your risk of a variety of problems and may even be immune healthy. Keep in mind that if you increase your intake of fiber, you should also increase your consumption of water, especially when taking a fiber supplement.

Some benefits of increasing fiber consumption are:
- Helps with weight control because it delays the emptying of stomach contents, delays the absorption of fats, and promotes a feeling of fullness.
- Improves glucose or sugar balance by delaying the movement and absorption of carbohydrates into the small intestine, so you simply burn your dietary fuel more efficiently and evenly.

- Reduces cholesterol levels by binding with cholesterol-carrying products in the intestine and causing it to be excreted or eliminated.
- Increases the weight of the stool and softens the stool to promote regular and smooth bowel movements.
- Reduces the colon transit time and pressure within the colon.
- Reduces the risk of a number of digestive conditions—diverticulitis, irritable bowel syndrome (IBS), hemorrhoids, and gastroesophageal reflux disease (GERD)—and promotes increases in healthy bacteria in the colon to improve overall digestive health.
- Reduces blood pressure and may reduce a man's PSA blood test number by lowering cholesterol.

I do not recommend most fiber dietary supplements and powders because they mostly contain only soluble fiber, which can create too much bloating and gas and you may have to take up to 50 pills a day to get your daily intake of fiber. The simplest way to boost your fiber intake is to eat a cereal in the morning and add flaxseed, small fruits, or other simple fiber sources (oat bran) to it. For example, my bran cereal gives me 13 to 15 grams of fiber per bowl. I add several tablespoons of flaxseed and I have almost 20 grams of fiber in one meal. I have almost reached my daily requirement in just one bowl of cereal! For the rest of the day, you can get additional fiber from some fruits and vegetables, bean products, nuts and seeds, whole grains, and even fiber bars. However, look for the fiber bar that is lowest in calories, sodium, and unhealthy fats and highest in insoluble fiber. I recommend mostly insoluble fiber because, unlike soluble fiber, it does not cause excess gas production in the bowel but still gives you the benefits of fiber.

Your Goal *Eating 20 to 30 grams of fiber a day is a good thing.*

WHAT ABOUT DIET PLANS—LOW-CARB, MEDITERRANEAN, LOW-FAT, WEIGHT WATCHERS®?

Talk to your doctor or a nutritionist about these diets, but most depend on lowering your intake of calories and exercising more. Regardless, your primary goal is to maintain a healthy weight, cholesterol, and blood pressure, and one diet or program does not necessarily work for everyone. Programs like Weight Watchers® are good because they teach you about food, moderation, and portion sizes. An added benefit is that they also involve a support group. Low carbohydrate diets may work for some individuals, but long-term they can be difficult to follow.

I generally like the Mediterranean diet because it is a moderate and diverse diet with many components. It is flexible, realistic, and practical to follow. For example, a typical Mediterranean diet consists of high monounsaturated and polyunsaturated, and low saturated fat intake, moderate alcohol intake, high consumption of bean products and fiber, cereals, fruits and vegetables, low consumption of meat and meat products, and a moderate intake of milk and dairy products. Basically, this is an "everything in moderation" diet.

A study was conducted by the National Cancer Institute and involved about 380,000 men and women following a Mediterranean pattern diet. It showed an impact on not just cardiovascular disease but cancers deaths. This dietary pattern has also been associated with lower risks of eye diseases and many others conditions, such as Alzheimer's disease.

Your Goal *Work with your health professional to develop a diet or dietary program that makes sense for you. Keep in mind that if it sounds too good to be true then it probably is. Your health professional should monitor your major indicators, including cholesterol, blood pressure, weight loss, and PSA level while you are on a new type of diet just to make sure it is working for you.*

THE TRUTH ABOUT SODIUM AND ALCOHOL

Let's clear the air quickly on the sodium subject. One of the largest government-funded studies in the history of medicine was called the DASH (Dietary Approaches to Stop Hypertension) study. The great thing about this original study was that it involved pre-hypertensive people not taking prescription medications. Half of the participants were women and 60 percent were African-Americans, and this also made the study remarkable. In analyzing results of this study, it was amazing to find that eating healthy and lowering sodium intake had a wonderfully positive impact on blood pressure numbers.

Currently, it is recommended that a healthy individual gets 2,300 milligrams of sodium (1 teaspoon) per day but, in the DASH diet, the effective dose was 1,500 milligrams of sodium per day. (Many people are regularly consuming 3,500 to 4,500 milligrams per day!) The DASH participants experienced an average drop in blood pressure of 11 mmHg systolic and 6 mmHg diastolic—a drop this large is generally obtained by using blood pressure–reducing medications.

Since about 80 percent of your daily sodium intake comes from processed foods and only about 5 percent from the salt-shaker, it is very important to carefully check the sodium content on nutritional labels. Don't be fooled by products marked "lower sodium." A quick look at some average sodium contents gives you an idea of how much they may vary for a particular product. Read your labels carefully!

- Breads   100–200 mg of sodium in 1 ounce.
- Chicken with rice soup (condensed)   600–1,300 mg of sodium in 1/2 cup.
- Frozen pizza (plain)   400–1,200 mg of sodium in 4 ounces.
- Frozen vegetables   5–150 mg of sodium in 1/2 cup.
- Potato chips   100 to 200 mg of sodium in 1 ounce.
- Pretzels   250 to 600 mg of sodium in 1 ounce.
- Salad dressing (regular)   50 to 250 mg of sodium in 1 tablespoon.
- Salsa   75 to 150 mg of sodium in 1 tablespoon.
- Soda   10 to 100 mg of sodium in 8 ounces.
- Tomato juice   350 to 1,000 mg of sodium in 8 ounces.
- Tomato soup   600 to 1,300 mg of sodium in 1/2 cup.

Now, on to alcohol. All types of alcohol (beer, hard liquor, red wine, white wine) in moderation may be healthy, but in excess all types of alcohol are unhealthy. Red wine has never been proven to be healthier than any other type of alcoholic drink (it has just been effectively marketed), and all forms of alcohol in excess are equally dangerous.

Let's review a "serving" of alcohol:
- One serving of beer = 12 ounces (about 13.2 grams of alcohol).
- One serving of hard alcohol = 1.5 ounce shot of 80 proof liquor (15.1 grams of alcohol).
- One serving of wine = 4–6 ounces (about 10.8 to 15 grams of alcohol).
- 1 gram of alcohol = about 7 calories.

Now, it is important to understand what is meant by "moderate amounts of alcohol"—for women one serving a day, and for men, one to two servings of alcohol per day.

Let's consider what alcohol in moderation may do for you:
- Increase good cholesterol or HDL
- Improve bone health
- Reduce your risk of a heart attack or stroke (may thin your blood or reduce stickiness of clot-forming platelets, reduce fibrinogen)
- Improve mental health
- May improve prostate health and sexual function (controversial)

Alcohol in excess can cause many problems, including:
- Increases triglycerides
- Increases sugar levels
- Increases the risk of osteoporosis
- Large source of calories (weight gain)
- Increases blood pressure
- Damages the heart
- Suppresses the immune system
- Reduces folic acid concentrations and variety of other nutrients

- Increases the risk of some cancers—oral/esophageal and breast cancer and possibly many other cancers such as lung cancer.
- Reduces sexual performance

Your Goal *Reduce sodium intake to not more than 1,500 to 2,300 mg per day. Be sure to review nutritional labels to look for sodium, particularly in processed foods. Do not start drinking alcohol just for the health benefits but, if you do consume alcohol, limit your intake to one drink per day for women and one to two drinks per day for men.*

OTHER HEART-HEALTHY RECOMMENDATIONS

I could write hundreds of pages on other items that are heart healthy but there are just not enough pages in any book, magazine, or handout to cover all these things in detail. For example, quitting smoking makes sense, not only to reduce your risk of a potentially aggressive cancer, but also to increase your chances of living a long life.

I am frequently asked if smoking is a clear risk factor for prostate cancer. I generally do not think the association between smoking and prostate cancer even matters because smoking increases your overall risk of dying early. That should be important enough to make you want to not smoke. Also, smoking has been associated with a lower survival rate in men already diagnosed with many cancers, including prostate cancer. There are so many potential programs and methods to help you quit today that talking with your doctor about these issues makes more sense than ever before.

We'll end this chapter with a bottom line principle to guide you—when in doubt about what to eat or drink or what lifestyle changes to make, just keep in mind that heart healthy equals prostate healthy!

SUMMARY

To end the chapter, let's consider what steps you might take to assess and then improve your cardiovascular health. Following is a lifestyle test that I use whenever I speak to health-care professionals and patient groups. It helps illustrate the importance of making many small lifestyle changes as opposed to doing just one or two extremely healthy things. What is interesting is that the research behind this test came from over 50 countries around the world, and from men and women of all races, ages, and professions (including doctors). Give it a try and see how your lifestyle stacks up. If you answer "no" to the question, consider a health improvement goal to enter.

HEALTHY PERSONAL LIFESTYLE QUESTIONS

Score one point for every time you answer yes.

1. *I do NOT currently smoke cigarettes/cigars or use any tobacco products (chewing tobacco).*

   _____ Yes, I agree with the statement.

   What goal might improve your health and score?

   _____

   _____

   _____

   _____

2. *I have regular cholesterol screenings done and have a normal level and a normal hs-CRP test. (Check pages 8–9 for normal levels.)*

   _____ Yes, I agree with the statement.

   What goal might improve your health and score?

   _____

   _____

   _____

   _____

3. *I have my blood pressure checked regularly and have a normal pressure. (Check page 9 for normal levels.)*

   _____ Yes, I agree with the statement.

   What goal might improve your health and score?

   _____

   _____

   _____

   _____

4. *I have a normal blood glucose level and have NOT been diagnosed with diabetes.*

   _____ Yes, I agree with the statement.

   What goal might improve your health and score?

   _____

   _____

   _____

   _____

5. *I have a normal (not overweight or obese) waist circumference.*

_____ Yes, I agree with the statement.

What goal might improve your health and score?

_____

_____

_____

_____

6. *I do not currently have depression, high stress, or other mental health issues.*

_____ Yes, I agree with the statement.

What goal might improve your health and score?

_____

_____

_____

_____

7. *I eat several servings of fruits and vegetables per day.*

_____ Yes, I agree with the statement.

What goal might improve your health and score?

_____

_____

_____

_____

8. *I drink alcohol in moderation or not at all. (1 drink a day maximum for women and 1–2 maximum for men)*

_____ Yes, I agree with the statement.

What goal might improve your health and score?

_____

_____

_____

_____

9. *I do at least 30 minutes of aerobic exercise per day on average.*

_____ Yes, I agree with the statement.

What goal might improve your health and score?

_____

_____

_____

10. *I lift weights or do some type of resistance exercise at least 2–3 times per week.*

_____ Yes, I agree with the statement.

What goal might improve your health and score?

_____

_____

_____

_____

Total Score _____

What does my score mean?

10 points = Congratulations!

7–9 points = Very Good! Keep up the good work and 10 points is within your reach!

4–6 points = Good! However, still a lot to work on.

1–3 points = Okay! Still need to make some major life changes very soon.

0 points = Need to change things now!

What does my score really mean in terms of health?

Men and women who lived the longest had the highest number of moderate healthy lifestyle choices. If someone had almost 10, or all 10, "yes" answers, there was about a 70 percent chance that they would live to at least age 85 without mental or physical disability. Each positive lifestyle choice gave the individual a 5–10% decreased risk of dying young or suffering from a cardiovascular event (heart attack, for example). The more of the lifestyle changes that you are able to accomplish, the greater the chance that you will not only live a longer life, but a more high-quality life! Finally, keep in mind that if you have any of the above conditions (such as depression, elevated glucose, or high cholesterol levels), but they are currently under medical and lifestyle control, then you can change your answer to "yes."

References:

"INTERHEART Study." *Lancet* 2004; 364: 937–952.

"Framingham Heart Study." *Journal of American Geriatric Society 2005*; 53: 1944–1950.

"INTERHEART Study." *Journal of American Medical Association 2007*; 297: 286–94.

"Honolulu Heart Program & Asia Aging Study." *Journal of American Medical Association 2006*; 296: 2343–50.

"Physicians' Health Study." *Arch Internal Medicine 2008*; 168: 284–90.

Just a final reminder …
heart healthy = prostate healthy!

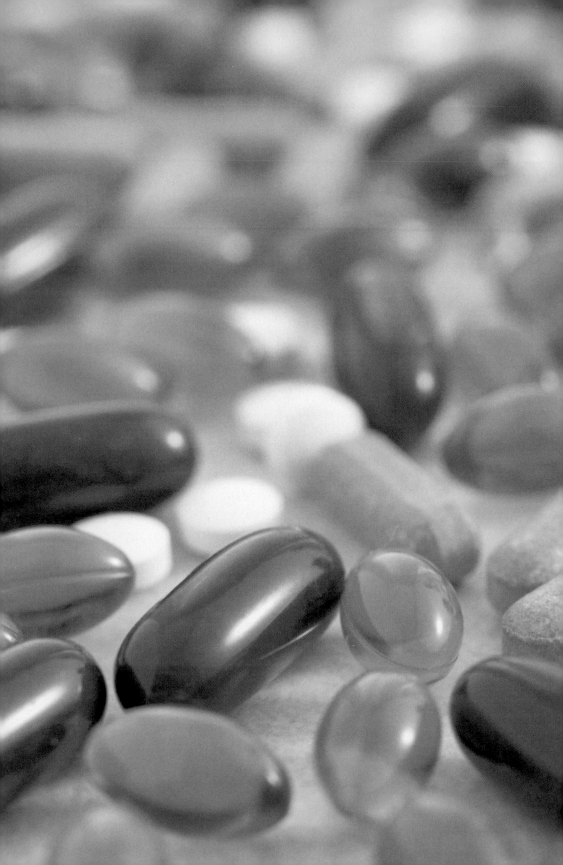

CHAPTER 2

Medications, Nutritional Supplements, and Other Healthy Suggestions

Now that you have taken steps to make heart- and prostate-healthy lifestyle changes, you are ready to consider what medications, supplements, and other healthy practices may be of value to you. We've attempted to provide general information on some of the most common ones considered of use to prostate cancer patients. This information should give you a starting point for discussions with your health-care provider on which of the practices would be good choices for your personal situation. You should always consult with your doctor before starting to take a particular supplement.

When it comes to any dietary supplement, I believe less is more and megadoses are never better. Every individual supplement that I have ever researched comes with serious side effects when taken in mega or large doses beyond what is truly needed. In fact, many megadose supplement studies suggest a worse outcome or prognosis in patients with cancer. In other words, talk to your doctor about whether or not you actually qualify for any pill based on your medical history and from the results of your latest medical tests. If you do qualify, talk to your doctor about the precise dose, frequency, and form or brand name of the supplement that was used in the best objective clinical studies that suggested a benefit. This is exactly the same standard doctors use for prescription medications, and dietary supplements should be treated in the same manner.

ASPIRIN (Low dose of 81 to 100 milligrams)

Low-dose aspirin continues to be one of the most promising over-the-counter products (OTCs) to reduce the risk of cardiovascular disease (heart attack and ischemic stroke, for example). There is some human research to suggest that aspirin may reduce the risk and progression of several cancers, including breast, colon, and even prostate cancer. However, many people take aspirin without truly qualifying for this medication and, in that case, the risk of side effects may outweigh the benefits. Never just start taking aspirin to prevent or treat cancer or even heart disease without talking to your doctor. I like to see at least some type of risk-to-benefit calculation, such as a Framingham Risk Score (go to the American Heart Association web site, www.americanheart.org, for more information), completed before starting aspirin treatment. Men who do NOT have an increased risk for ulcers and/or internal bleeding, normal or low blood pressure (with or without medication), and have a 1-year risk of a cardiovascular event that is around 10 percent (from the Framingham risk score) are potential candidates. Regular or daily use of non-steroidal anti-inflammatory drugs (NSAIDs), such as ibuprofen or Motrin®, or prescription COX-2 inhibitor drugs such as Celebrex® and others, should NOT be used for prostate cancer prevention or treatment unless approved by the primary care doctor or cardiologist, because the risk of side effects is generally greater than the benefits they can provide for you.

B-VITAMIN DIETARY SUPPLEMENTS
(including B1, B2, B3, B6, B12, and Folic Acid)

Over the past 10 years, numerous clinical trials were started in the hope that high doses of B vitamins could reduce the risk of cardiovascular disease and even cancer. However, researchers have been surprised to learn that they may actually promote heart disease and encourage the growth of cancer at megadoses. Many cancers, including prostate cancer, have receptors for large doses of B vitamins, especially folic acid. In other words, researchers believe that these tumors use vitamins as nutrients to help them grow, so to speak. The large clinical trials have simply suggested that "less is more" when it comes to megadosing with vitamins and minerals.

The only B vitamin that needs to be taken in higher doses by some individuals with heart disease is vitamin B3, which is also known as "niacin." This B-vitamin can increase HDL and lower LDL and triglycerides, and it can be used with a statin drug and most other heart medications. Niacin comes in a prescription or an over-the-counter version. It is heart healthy, but does come with side effects, which is why only some individuals qualify for it.

On rare occasions, some people may also qualify for slightly higher doses of B12 or folic acid because their blood level is so low that it can cause problems with their health. Regardless, most individuals reading this book need to just stick to healthy food and a low-dose multivitamin once daily to get their recommended daily allowance of B vitamins.

CALCIUM AND VITAMIN D

Since they relate to each other so closely and both are crucial to bone health, we'll consider them together. Calcium, vitamin D, and weight lifting do reduce bone fractures as long as you can take your dietary supplement pills (about 80 percent of the time) and exercise regularly. Bone health is not only an issue with some testosterone-reducing treatments for prostate cancer, but it is fast becoming a serious concern for men in general as they get older. In fact, although bone health and bone fractures are much more common in women than men, it is now an accepted medical fact that men have a greater chance of dying from a bone fracture as compared to women. Therefore, bone health has also become a major men's health issue.

Let's review the approximate requirements for total calcium (mg) and vitamin D (IU-international units) daily intake, combining diet and supplements. Keep in mind that, regardless of the adult's age, the average dietary intake of calcium is about 600 mg to 800 mg per day at best.

Calcium and Vitamin D Requirements

AGE	CALCIUM (MG)	VITAMIN D
19–49 years	1,000	200 IU (5 mcg)
50–70 years	1,200	400 IU (10 mcg)
Over 70 years	1,200	600 IU (15 mcg)

Sources: Surgeon General's Report on Bone Health and Osteoporosis and National Academy of Sciences.

As you can see from the chart, men generally need a daily total of 1,000 to 1,200 milligrams from foods, beverages, and/or supplements. Your doctor should determine the specific amount of calcium needed because that amount may vary depending on test results. However, it is important to understand that much of the calcium you consume from food or beverages is not completely absorbed by the body. The amount absorbed may be about only 33–50 percent of the amount ingested. This may sound a little frustrating, but you can easily reach your calcium goal by getting some additional calcium from a supplement.

Calcium Rich Foods
- Collard greens 360 mg
- Orange juice (fortified) 350 mg
- Sardines 325 mg
- Oatmeal (instant) 325 mg
- Yogurt 300 mg
- Milk 300 mg
- Cheese 270 mg

After you are able to determine your absorbed dietary calcium intake, you may want to consider dietary supplements. Calcium supplements are not only generally safe but are effective at reducing the risk of fractures. *However, if they are not taken regularly (about 24–25 days of every month), they simply do not work in many cases.*

Before a commercial gets to you, please make sure that you learn about the positives and negatives of each supplement type. In general, the higher percentage of elemental calcium by weight, the more beneficial the product.

Ideally, calcium dietary supplements should be taken in divided doses throughout the day, because the human body generally absorbs approximately 500 mg of elemental calcium at a time. If you take more than this at once, you will not absorb as much as if you spread the dosages out. Check for the amount of "elemental calcium" in each tablet, because this is the form of calcium that is absorbed and actually counted for the required daily calcium intake. Some of the supplements may also contain vitamin D, which increases capsule/tablet size just a little. You may want to get vitamin D from a separate supplement or source in order to reduce the size of the pill you are taking. You do not need to have

TYPE OF CALCIUM SUPPLEMENT	ELEMENTAL CALCIUM BY WEIGHT	COMMENTS
Calcium carbonate	40%	My first choice: most tested; requires fewest pills/day; can be used as an acid reflux drug. Least expensive. Should be taken with food because you need some stomach acid to absorb these supplements, in general.
Calcium phosphate	38% or 31%	My second choice: fewer pills to take, in general. Tricalcium or dicalcium phosphate. Can be taken with or without food. Simplicity and price getting closer to calcium carbonate. Need many more clinical trials before they will be recommended on a regular basis.
Calcium citrate or Calcium citrate malate	21%	My third choice: better absorbed, especially in a low-acid stomach environment so it can be taken with or without food. More expensive & more pills needed daily, so long-term compliance is an issue.

vitamin D in your calcium supplement for better absorption.

Let's spend a bit more time on vitamin D. It is important to consider one blood test that is fairly inexpensive and may tell you and your doctor about your risk of a future fracture. This is the vitamin D blood test. Normal blood levels of vitamin D are needed to maintain proper bone health. The 25-hydroxy-vitamin D (25-OH vitamin D) test is the preferred test for most patients, but a second test may also be used in patients with abnormal kidney function. Experts agree that normal results for a 25-OH vitamin D test are approximately 35–40 ng/ml or 90–100 nmol/L. Some tests may run a little higher or lower, but this is a good goal for men concerned about bone loss. Some advocates are calling for really high vitamin D blood levels, for example 60 ng/ml (150 nmol/L) or higher, but I do not support this recommendation. I have never seen a situation where more is indeed better when there is no good human research to support the belief. Regardless, what all of this means is that most people would need to take about 800 to 1,000 IU (or more) just to achieve a normal blood level of vitamin D. I suggest that you let the 25-OH vitamin D test result and your doctor's advice help you to decide how much vitamin D you need to take daily. Keep in mind that the test is most accurate when it is done in the late fall or winter time, because this is when vitamin D levels tend to be the lowest (due to less ultraviolet B light exposure from the sun). However, if necessary, the test can be done any time of the year.

If your blood test results suggest that you need more vitamin D, it can be obtained from the following sources:

- Fortified beverages and foods—milk, soy, protein bars, and cereal. Only eggs, mushrooms, and seafood contain vitamin D naturally, but varieties of other beverages and foods are fortified with vitamin D. Check the label on the product to determine the amount.
- Fish and fish oils—Fish and some fish oil supplements contain a high level of vitamin D.

FISH SOURCE	VITAMIN D
Salmon (wild)	1,000 IU (25 mcg)
Oysters	545 IU (14 mcg)
Catfish	425 IU (11 mcg)
Bluefish	415 IU (10 mcg)
Mackerel	395 IU (10 mcg)

Be careful with some supplements because they may also contain very high levels of vitamin A, which can be bone unhealthy.

- Multivitamin or an individual vitamin D supplement—most contain at least 400 IU of vitamin D.
- Prescription drugs—Calcitriol and other vitamin D sources can be prescribed and taken orally or given as an injection if the doctor thinks you need to get vitamin D from these sources.

■ Sun (ultraviolet B light) 10–15 minutes of sunlight several times per week, especially during the spring and summer, allows the human body to make some vitamin D. Sunscreen users, African Americans, overweight, and older individuals have a more difficult time making this vitamin.

Keep in mind that, in general, 100 IU (2.5 mcg) of vitamin D per day is needed just to raise your blood level about 1 ng/ml (2.5 nmol/L) after 2–3 months. So, if you need to raise your blood level 4 ng/ml (10 nmol/L) you would need to take 400 IU (10 mcg) of vitamin D per day. If you need to raise your level 10 ng/ml (25 nmol/L), you guessed it, you would need 1,000 IU (25 mcg) of vitamin D per day for 2–3 months. The bottom line is that after you normalize your vitamin D blood test, 800 to 1,000 IU of vitamin D per day should help to maintain it unless directed otherwise by your doctor based on blood test results.

There are basically two types of vitamin D supplements available for over-the-counter purchase—vitamin D2 (also known as "ergocalciferol") and vitamin D3 (also known as "cholecalciferol"). Vitamin D3 is the type that most experts believe should be taken if you have a choice. Some of the many reasons vitamin D3 is preferred are: vitamin D3 is the form that humans make naturally from sunlight and the type found in wild fish; it is just as cost effective as vitamin D2 and raises the blood test results better than D2; and vitamin D3 has been used in most of the human studies to prevent bone loss in men and women.

Whether or not you should take calcium and vitamin D supplements is dependent on whether or not you qualify for these pills. To see if you qualify for calcium supplements, you should ideally determine how much calcium you get from dietary sources working with a nutritionist, and to see how much vitamin D you need you should work with the blood test and your doctor.

CHOLESTEROL-, BLOOD PRESSURE–, AND SUGAR-LOWERING PRESCRIPTION MEDICATIONS

The amazing thing about cholesterol-lowering medications (statins) is that they not only seem to reduce the risk of cardiovascular disease, but they recently have been associated with better prostate health and may improve your prognosis during and after treatment for prostate cancer. Statins may also increase vitamin D blood levels. The same findings have been suggested for blood pressure and sugar-reducing (diabetes) medications. This requires further study. If you cannot get your cholesterol, blood pressure, or sugar levels down to normal levels with healthy lifestyle changes, then do not be shy about asking your doctor about some of these medications that may help.

There is a dietary supplement known as "red yeast rice extract" that has helped reduce cholesterol in the small number of individuals who are not able to take any of the statin medications. However, this dietary supplement contains one of the active ingredients found in an actual statin, so patients on this supplement should be monitored (liver and muscle enzyme studies) as if they are on a statin. However, I generally recommend statins because they have the clinical research, are covered by insurance, and have a great safety record.

DUTASTERIDE, FINASTERIDE (5-alpha-reductase inhibitors) & OTHER BPH (alpha-blockers) PRESCRIPTION MEDICATIONS

New research is emerging to suggest dutasteride and finasteride, also known as the "5-alpha-reductase inhibitors," may not only reduce your risk of prostate cancer but may help to partially treat the disease along with conventional treatment. In the meantime, these drugs are used in some men with noncancerous enlargement of the prostate or benign prostatic hyperplasia (BPH) because they actually shrink the prostate over time and work especially well in men with large prostates. Dutasteride and finasteride can reduce a man's PSA level by up to 50 percent over six months. However, whether or not these pills can help treat prostate cancer as well as they can prevent prostate cancer is still controversial. You should talk to your doctor about the latest research on these and other BPH medications because numerous large clinical trials are going on now in the prevention and treatment setting. Finasteride at 5 mg per day is used for BPH in some patients, but the same drug at 1 mg per day is approved by numerous countries to prevent hair loss or premature balding! Even at the 1 mg per day dosage, it can reduce a man's PSA level, so the bottom line is that you should tell your doctor if you are taking any of these medications.

Another class of BPH medications known as "alpha-blockers" relaxes the prostate in men with BPH and may have some cancer-preventive effects. These drugs generally work faster to improve urinary problems in men with BPH, but their anti-cancer effects are not as well established and they do not generally cause a large reduction in PSA. Some men with severe BPH take both types of drugs to help relieve their symptoms, but the vast majority of men with BPH take one or the other drug.

Some of the herbal prostate enlargement supplements like saw palmetto have a good safety record and may provide a little benefit, but the prescription medications for BPH work so well and may help to prevent and treat some prostate cancers that they are obviously a better choice. If you want to take an herbal BPH supplement with your prescription drug, talk to your doctor about this possibility.

FIBER-BASED DIETARY SUPPLEMENTS

Although discussed briefly in the first chapter, I thought it worth considering here as well. There is little need to spend money on fiber pills because they require anywhere from 30 to 60 pills a day to reach the recommended daily allowance for fiber. Save your money. Fiber powders, wafers, and crackers are not inexpensive and most contain the type of fiber that can cause a lot of gas and bloating. Fiber-based or bran and oatmeal-based cereal or porridge with ground flaxseed on top is a good way to get your fiber, reduce your cholesterol, and hopefully your PSA level. However, if you do prefer a fiber bar, look for one that is generally less than 150 calories and contains about 10 grams of mostly insoluble fiber.

FISH OIL (Omega-3 fatty acids)

Several studies have suggested that taking fish oil pills containing the two primary fish oils, EPA and DHA (500 mg–1 gram per day), may reduce the risk of sudden cardiac death and may reduce the risk of other cardiovascular events. In addition, fish oil may reduce triglycerides, which may be increased in men on some treatments for prostate cancer, and may have anti-arthritic and anti-cancer properties as well as other important benefits. Fish oil pills also tend to be low in mercury. However, keep in mind that even fish oils come with a catch. They may thin your blood too much and increase your risk of internal bleeding. Please discuss with your doctor whether or not you qualify for a fish oil supplement. Individuals already on another blood-thinning medication have to be careful when combining it with fish oil pills.

LYCOPENE

Sources of Lycopene

Tomatoes
   and tomato
   products
Watermelon
Guava
Pink grapefruit
Papaya
Apricots

There have been only a few studies of men taking lycopene supplements for prostate cancer prevention or with conventional treatment, and the results thus far are inconclusive and controversial. More studies are desperately needed, but in the meantime if you want to take a low-dose lycopene supplement please talk to your doctor first. I am not a big supporter of lycopene dietary supplements for prostate cancer, but generally suggest getting more lycopene from food rather than supplements at this time.

MULTIVITAMINS

One Pill a Day Maximum of an Inexpensive
Children's or Women's Low–Dose Multivitamin

One of the largest studies of men taking a single pill, low-dose multivitamin once a day seemed to show it prevented prostate cancer, but another study showed that men taking 2 or more multivitamin pills a day had a higher risk for advanced and fatal prostate cancer! In other words, less is more when it comes to multivitamins. It is possible that higher doses of these pills may feed prostate tumors. The real problem is that many men's multivitamins contain too high a concentration of antioxidants. Taking a women's multivitamin without iron or simply a children's multivitamin several times a week, not to exceed one multivitamin pill a day, makes sense.

Individuals can use the following guide to determine if their multivitamin contains too much or too little of key ingredients. Remember that the percent daily value (% DV) or the Recommended Daily Allowance (RDA) should be the maximum (not the minimum) amount of the ingredient you need in your multivitamin, in my opinion.

VITAMIN/ MINERAL/ NUTRIENT	MAXIMUM DOSAGE NEEDED (GENERALLY 50 TO 100% DV OR RDA) PER DAILY PILL	THE AMOUNT IN YOUR MULTIVITAMIN (WRITE IN THE SPACE PROVIDED)
Vitamin A	2,500 to 5,000 IU	
Vitamin C	60 to 120 mg	
Vitamin D	At least 400 to 800 IU (10 to 20 mcg)	
Vitamin E	15 to 30 IU	
Vitamin K	20 to 80 mcg	
Vitamin B1 (Thiamine)	1 to 1.5 mg	
Vitamin B2 (Riboflavin)	1 to 2 mg	
Niacin (Vitamin B3)	20 mg	
Vitamin B6 (Pyridoxine)	2 mg	
Vitamin B12 (Cobalamin)	6 mcg	
Folic Acid	400 mcg	
Biotin	30 to 150 mcg	
Pantothenic Acid	10 mg	
Calcium	At least 200 to 500 mg	
Iodine	150 mcg	
Magnesium	50 to 100 mg	
Zinc	10 to 15 mg	
Selenium	20 to 100 mcg	
Copper	2 mg	
Manganese	2 mg	
Molybdenum	80 mcg	

Note: Only calcium and vitamin D should be found in larger amounts because men need them for better bone health. Please be most careful about folic acid and zinc in higher amounts than the DV or RDA, because they have been associated with a higher risk of aggressive prostate cancer in some of the largest human studies. Be especially careful of any multivitamin that asks you to take more than one pill a day. Also, try to find a multivitamin that does not contain herbal products, because they could interfere with your treatment.

PROBIOTIC DIETARY SUPPLEMENTS

Probiotics are the so-called friendly bacteria that are advertised for immune health and promoted by some companies as being completely safe. Friendly bacteria do have a good track record for safety in foods that carry them, such as yogurt or a yogurt drink. However, using a probiotic dietary supplement recently became a concern when patients with pancreatic problems (pancreatitis) were found to have a greater risk of dying from their condition when getting a variety of daily probiotic supplements as compared to a placebo.

My rule of thumb is that I do not consider any pill safe for a prostate cancer patient unless it has been tested in prostate cancer patients specifically. Probiotics in food seem fine, but we have no idea if taking these supplements after being diagnosed with cancer can help, harm, or do nothing. Also, getting millions of these bacteria may overwhelm your immune system and not stimulate it. You need a strong immune system to fight your prostate cancer, particularly because many of our best conventional medicines rely on a person having a normal immune system.

One exception is bladder cancer where, in some clinical studies, preliminary results indicate that Lactobacillus casei (a probiotic) may help along with conventional treatment. For a variety of reasons, bladder cancer was the most likely cancer that could benefit from these pills. Regardless, after the pancreatic study, I simply am not a supporter of probiotic supplements for patients diagnosed with or treated for prostate cancer until someone can show that they are safe and actually help.

QUERCETIN (for chronic nonbacterial prostatitis)

This is a compound found in grapes, garlic, and other natural sources, which has some anti-inflammatory properties. We have no idea if it helps to prevent or treat prostate cancer, but it has been used with some success in treating chronic nonbacterial prostatitis. This type of pain and inflammation of the prostate is more common than previously realized. One of the most clinically tested and utilized products in the world is Q-Urol (www.Q-urol.com). However, first check with your doctor to see if you even qualify for it. It is not uncommon to combine quercetin with prescription medication for chronic nonbacterial prostatitis. Quercetin is also being studied for blood pressure reduction, but it is too early to know if it has any major impact in these areas.

SAW PALMETTO & OTHER BPH DIETARY SUPPLEMENTS

This is one of the most popular herbal products around the world used to provide some relief for the symptoms of benign prostatic hyperplasia (BPH). In one of the largest, most recent, and best clinical trials in the world, the most commonly used dosage (320 mg per day) was very safe but worked no better than a placebo. However, a placebo works well for some men with mild BPH (no kidding). Higher doses (500 mg to 1,000 mg a day) are being tested right now for BPH. There is no strong human research using saw palmetto to prevent or treat prostate cancer. There is a concern that higher doses of saw palmetto may artificially reduce PSA blood levels and, in my opinion, this can happen in some men at the higher doses. Other, less popular BPH herbal products or natural remedies such as beta-sitosterol, pygeum africanum, rye pollen, and stinging nettle do not have as much research as saw palmetto and need to be tested more to see if they work better than a placebo. The biggest problem that all of these herbal products have is that the prescription medications for BPH work so well today (and they may even prevent prostate cancer and hair loss) that it is difficult to ever consider recommending an herbal product over a drug for this prostate problem. Most men who use the herbal supplement take it along with prescription medication, with their doctor's approval, of course.

SCREENING FOR OTHER DISEASES/CONDITIONS

Abdominal Aortic Aneurysm, Colon Cancer, Depression, Skin Cancer

These may seem strange to consider in a chapter mostly dedicated to medications and supplements, but several screening tests are so important to maintaining well being that they deserve a mention here.

Colon cancer is the third most common cause of cancer death in men (after prostate cancer). Screening for colon cancer with a colonoscopy, for example, has the potential to cure you during the actual screening procedure. Doctors can remove colon polyps during the procedure in some cases, and this can help to reduce your risk of developing colon cancer. Imagine if all of the cancer screening tests allowed you to be potentially cured while the doctor was screening you for the disease. Generally, men and women age 50 and older qualify for colon cancer screening. If there is a family history of the disease, some doctors like to start screening at the age of 40, and I could not agree more with this. There are several different methods used for colon cancer screening, from testing for blood in the stool, to laboratory testing, to imaging, to sigmoidoscopy and colonoscopy. Ask your doctor about the screening test that is right for you, but for most individuals I recommend a colonoscopy.

Mental health has to be as important as physical health. There is also enough research now to suggest that one impacts the other and vice versa. I am a big advocate of attempting to improve your mental health, particularly if you and your doctor believe it is an issue. I think it is interesting that, when someone is diagnosed with prostate cancer or any cancer, seeking multiple opinions to improve your physical health is accepted today as normal. However, seeking the advice of a mental health expert is not as routine. Why? We have to accept the fact that for some men and women dealing with a cancer, the situation can be stressful and the impact on one's mental health should be a priority.

At least in some countries, a new screening test approved for men aged 65–75 years who have ever smoked is abdominal aortic aneurysm (AAA) screening. It is done one time with an ultrasound, a device that is safe and gives off no radiation. Talk to your doctor to see if you qualify.

Other important screening tests—hearing, sight, skin cancer, and others—need to be handled on an individual basis. There are so many screening tests today that deciding which ones are important for an individual should be based on discussions with a trusted doctor. High priority screenings will focus on what has the greatest chance of reducing one's quality and quantity of life. The screening tests mentioned above are endorsed by the U.S. Preventive

Services Task Force and other authoritative preventive agencies.

Finally, there should be a quick note about what I call "spirituality screening," but this is not intended to be a religious statement. This just means that I firmly believe that once in while we need to ask ourselves what we are doing for our fellow human beings when it comes to better health because there is so much that needs to be done. For example, volunteering for your favorite charity, donating time and money, or simply encouraging others to also volunteer can change someone's life. There are many wonderful prostate cancer organizations that need your help and a list of them is found at the end of this book.

SELENIUM

In one of the only studies of selenium versus a sugar pill (placebo), selenium supplements (200 mcg/day) were associated with a lower risk of prostate cancer. However, talk to your doctor first about whether or not you should go on an individual selenium supplement. Fish, garlic, Brazil nuts, and numerous other heart-healthy foods contain a lot of selenium. Ideally, a selenium blood test or a toenail clippings test (where you actually send toenail clippings to the laboratory—no kidding here) is the best way to determine whether or not you should go on an individual selenium supplement. The blood test measures selenium intake over the past 2 to 3 months, and the toenail clippings test measures your selenium intake over the past 9 to 12 months (talk to your doctor about which one is cheaper and better for you if you are interested in being tested). If the results of your blood or nail clippings selenium test are abnormally low, then one possibility is to first increase consumption of foods that have a lot of selenium. If your selenium levels continue to be low, then the next possibility is to add an individual supplement to your diet. Some multivitamins contain 100 or more micrograms of selenium, and this is generally enough without having to take an individual supplement.

TEA AND TEA SUPPLEMENTS

Most forms of tea, including black, green, herbal, and oolong, are healthy and have little or no calories, so enjoy drinking them.

However, please keep in mind that tea-based dietary supplements or pills (not the drink) have no solid proof from human studies that they do anything against prostate cancer. A large clinical trial of high-dose green tea supplements in patients with advanced cancer showed no real benefit. Patients on warfarin (a prescription blood thinner) should be careful to avoid getting large amounts of green tea because it can be a significant source of vitamin K and can reduce the efficacy of this popular blood-thinning drug.

TESTOSTERONE-LOWERING SUPPLEMENTS
(PC-SPES and others)

If your PSA drops significantly over a short period of time after taking a dietary supplement, talk to your doctor about getting a total testosterone and/or estrogen (estradiol) blood test. Over the last 15 years, I have witnessed several expensive dietary supplements contaminated with high concentrations of estrogen and/or estrogen-like plants that simply reduce testosterone and/or increase estrogen and thus cause a large drop in PSA over a short time. The problem with these supplements is that they not only can cost you a lot of money but they can also be life threatening in some cases. There is such a large amount of estrogen-like material in some of these non-regulated pills that they increase breast size, cause breast pain, and increase the risk of blood clots and death. Basically, these are a costly scam or rip-off! Stay away from them, please. In the United States and around the world, there are several instances of this problem. For example, in the United States there was a dietary supplement called "PC-SPES," which cost patients thousands of dollars in some cases and caused some of the earlier mentioned side effects. It was later found through laboratory analysis to be contaminated with some prescription drugs and contained high amounts of estrogen-like compounds. It was removed from the market but numerous similar products have filled the marketplace, so be careful, please.

VACCINES

Another side topic, but an important one! Talk to your doctor about updating your vaccines, because this could improve both the quality and quantity of your life. In my opinion, the flu, pneumococcal, and shingles vaccines are commonly missed in men with prostate cancer. Here is a list of some of the vaccines you can review with your primary care doctor:

- Flu shot (influenza vaccine): once a year in the early fall season, if age 50 years or older, or earlier if in a risk group (diabetes, heart disease, immune issues). In my opinion, most individuals diagnosed with prostate cancer should talk to their doctor about this vaccine, because the flu and pneumonia cause 36,000 deaths and 200,000 hospitalizations a year in the United States alone. In addition, the immune boost that is derived from this vaccine may provide other health benefits, and this is true of the other vaccines.
- Hepatitis A and/or B: if in a risk group
- Measles-mumps-rubella vaccine: once, if born after 1956 and not immune
- Pneumococcal vaccine: at age 65 or sooner if risk factors are present
- Shingles vaccine: if age 60 years or older (or earlier if in a high-risk group) and you never had shingles, some individuals may qualify even if they have had shingles.
- Tetanus-diphtheria (Td) booster: every 10 years
- Varicella (Chicken Pox) vaccine: if not immune

VITAMIN C

Ascorbic acid or vitamin C is the most famous and one of the most popular dietary supplements around the world, but researchers have no strong idea yet if it has any impact on helping to prevent or treat any type of cancer. In one of the largest cancer prevention trials, a moderate dosage (120 mg) of vitamin C along with several other nutrients may have helped to reduce risk in men over others who had a lower intake of this vitamin. In addition, there has been some interest in getting megadoses (1000s of milligrams) of this vitamin from pills or even intravenously from a doctor, but the research that this may help is weak, and it can cost you a fortune. Most of the studies of megadoses used patients with advanced or even terminal cancer and, in some cases, it made patients feel better, but it had no impact on improving their survival rate. Also, the research on vitamin C to improve immune health or reduce the risk of cold or lung infection has seen the most benefit at a moderate dosage (about 500 mg per day).

VITAMIN E

Fifty IU or less (in fact, in most non-smokers, only 15 to 30 mg or IU) of vitamin E is enough to normalize blood levels.

ZINC & OTHER EYE-HEALTH SUPPLEMENTS

This mineral has been promoted as an eye-healthy, immune-healthy, and prostate-healthy dietary supplement. However, zinc supplements in high dosages, 80 to 100 mg/day or more, should be avoided by most men and women, in my opinion. Recent human research has linked higher doses of zinc from dietary supplements to abnormal immune changes, a potential reduction in the impact of bone-building drugs, abnormal changes in the cholesterol blood tests, increased risk of urinary tract infections, kidney stones, prostate enlargement, and an increased risk of aggressive prostate cancer. Some government health organizations (Canada, for example) no longer allow the sale of high-dose zinc in a single pill based on this new research. Normally, only 0.5 mg of zinc is lost from the body every day, and this is easily replaced by dietary sources. Keep in mind that most good cheap multivitamins contain about 10–20 mg of zinc, which is more than enough for most men with just one exception.

Men taking zinc supplements for eye health, or more specifically the dry form of age-related macular degeneration (AMD), should not take more than 80 mg of zinc per day from these supplements. This was the dosage, along with other antioxidants (500 mg vitamin C, 400 IU vitamin E, 15 mg beta-carotene, and 2 mg cupric oxide), that may have reduced the risk of going blind in individuals with moderate to severe forms of AMD. So, if there is an issue of preserving your sight because of your AMD, your cancer and eye doctors should both agree first and foremost that you need zinc in higher doses, along with other antioxidants, before you take these eye-health supplements. Most individuals that I meet with around the world taking high-dose zinc or other high-dose antioxidants for eye health do not have moderate to severe AMD and should not be taking an eye-health dietary supplement.

OTHER SUPPLEMENTS

Please keep in mind that most other dietary supplements are not needed at this time. If you are interested in a unique supplement, you should discuss it with your health-care provider.

IMPORTANT NOTE: I generally advise that 2–3 weeks before any surgical or radiation procedure patients should discontinue the use of almost all dietary supplements. Preliminary evidence has demonstrated that some supplements may thin your blood during surgery, may interact with the anesthetic used in surgery, or may reduce the impact of radiation or other conventional treatments. Therefore, in order to be safe rather than sorry, it is best to focus on healthy lifestyle and dietary changes during this time. When you have recovered from surgery or have completed radiation or other conventional treatments, then you and your doctor should discuss when it is okay to restart the use of certain dietary supplements. This general rule should also apply to chemotherapy or other treatments. Always have a discussion with your doctor before conventional prostate cancer treatment begins about which supplements are and are not appropriate during this time. For example, some doctors advise vitamin D supplementation with some chemotherapy drugs and others do not. Again, as always, the ultimate decision about which dietary supplements to discontinue or maintain during conventional prostate cancer treatment should be between you and your doctor. Regardless, it is always beneficial to focus on healthy lifestyle changes during the time of conventional treatment (see chapter 1).

DIETARY SUPPLEMENTS TO CONSIDER WITH MY DOCTOR

After reviewing the chapter, you may want to select supplements that may be beneficial to your health and discuss them with your doctor at your next visit.

DIETARY SUPPLEMENT	DOSAGE & OTHER CONSIDERATIONS	REASON FOR TAKING

OTHER SCREENING TESTS I NEED:

_____

_____

_____

VACCINES I NEED:

_____

_____

_____

CHAPTER 3

From Diagnosis to Grading to Staging

This chapter is simply a quick guide to be used with your doctor in terms of discussing anything from the anatomy of the prostate gland to biopsy to grading (aggressiveness of your cancer) and staging (location of your cancer). It is a summary designed to help you better understand your prostate cancer, how it is acting, and where it may be located. Please use this material with your physician.

ANATOMY

Notice that the prostate sits deep in the pelvic area of the body (Figure A). It consists of 3 zones: the peripheral zone or PZ (65–70% of the total area of the prostate), the central zone or CZ (20–25% of the total area of the prostate), and the transition zone or TZ (5–10% of the total area of the prostate). Most prostate cancers begin growing in the PZ, and this is the area or zone that can be felt by the doctor during the digital rectal exam (DRE). The DRE only takes seconds. Prostate cancer less frequently grows in the CZ and TZ. The TZ surrounds the urethra or part of the body that carries urine from the bladder to the penis. The TZ is where benign prostatic hyperplasia (BPH) or non-cancerous enlargement of the prostate occurs, which is also common and can cause urinary problems. Please discuss with your health-care professional the specifics of prostate anatomy.

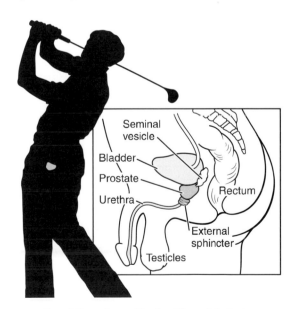

Figure A. The anatomy and location of the prostate gland.

BLOOD & URINE TESTS

There are several versions of the Prostate Specific Antigen (PSA) blood test and a new urine test that you and your doctor may want to discuss. The bottom line is that the lower the PSA value over time the better, and this includes before and after diagnosis and treatment. Keep in mind that every test, including the PSA, comes with a catch and you should ask the doctor what the catch is because no test is perfect.

PSA (Prostate Specific Antigen)

This blood test used to be considered normal when your PSA level was below 4 ng/ml, but newer research has revealed that a man can have cancer at any PSA level. Although it is more likely that cancer is involved with a higher PSA value, it should be kept in mind that BPH and even an infection of the prostate can raise the PSA level significantly. Therefore, many doctors are now relying on the way PSA changes over time (also known as "PSA kinetics") in combination with age, family history, race, weight, DRE, and, at times, imaging tests to determine if a man should have a biopsy or if there is a possibility that cancer is in the prostate. The value of PSA is not only checked before diagnosis, but especially after diagnosis and treatment.

PSA Density (PSAD = PSA/size of the prostate)

If you have had your PSA measured and have also received a transrectal ultrasound (TRUS) around the same time, this can help to determine your PSAD. TRUS, along with a DRE, is a good way to determine the size of the prostate and, when the PSA level is divided by the size or volume of the prostate, this equals PSAD. Some studies indicate that there is a greater chance of prostate cancer with a higher PSAD.

PSA Doubling Time

PSA doubling time is now viewed as important because it is the time it takes for your PSA value to double from your first PSA test. It can provide some valuable information before and after diagnosis or treatment. It can be calculated with just a few PSA tests over time, and you do not need to wait for your actual PSA to double in order to predict or calculate with your doctor how quickly it will double. The faster a PSA doubles, the more likely that your cancer is on the move.

PSA Velocity (PSAV)

This measurement is also relevant because it is the determination of how quickly the PSA is rising over a certain period of time. At least 2 to 3 individual PSA tests are needed over 6 months to a year to calculate this value. A higher PSAV over a period of time is more of an indication of cancer as compared to a low PSAV. For example, if your PSA goes from 1 to 3 ng/ml in one year (PSAV = 2), this is more of a concern compared to one that goes from 1 to 1.5 ng/ml (PSAV = 0.5). It can also provide valuable information about your cancer before and after treatment.

Free-to-Total PSA Blood Test

This test or a version of it can help the doctor decide if you need a biopsy when the situation is not quite clear. The greater the percentage of free PSA in the blood compared to PSA that is bound to something else, the greater the chance that you are "free" of cancer. So, a man with a free PSA of 35% is less likely to have cancer as compared to one who has a free PSA of 10%. Again, this test and the urine test described after this should only be used when the decision to biopsy or not is unclear.

Urine Tests (PCA3 and others)

There are several new urine tests (one test is known as "PCA3") that might help the doctor determine if you need a biopsy. In general, these urine tests are done in the office and may require some prostatic massage by the doctor to get a sample. The tests are usually offered for men whose PSA and other tests have not provided a clear enough idea of whether or not a biopsy is needed or if cancer might be present. The higher the score on the urine tests, the higher the chance that you have cancer.

OTHER TESTS

There are many other tests that a doctor can use to determine if or where a cancer may exist. For example, some doctors use a magnetic resonance imaging (MRI) or an Endorectal Coil MRI that may help to find cancer in and around the prostate if the blood, urine, or even biopsy has not revealed a complete picture of your situation. Other men may be offered a bone scan, a full body picture of your bones, if there is a concern that cancer may have spread to the bones. The bottom line is that there are lots of options that your doctor can use to determine if or where a cancer is located. Tests appropriate for your situation should be discussed further with your doctor.

THE PROSTATE BIOPSY

It is impossible for most individuals to be diagnosed with prostate cancer without a sample of prostate tissue or a biopsy (Figure B). The doctor will take numerous samples (also called "cores") from different areas of the prostate. The number of samples taken depends on your situation and your doctor. The standard number used to be 6, but better detection has been achieved by increasing the number of samples in some cases to 12 or more. Regardless of the number of samples, a pathologist reads them and decides whether each and every sample taken has normal cells, cancerous cells, and/or something that is not cancerous but is also not quite normal in appearance. Since a biopsy can reveal more than just cancer present, I recommend that every man keep a copy of the biopsy report. Figures C and D are examples of reports for a 6-core and a 12-core biopsy. Notice how the report not only shows the location of the sample that has cancer, but it also quantifies the percentage of the sample

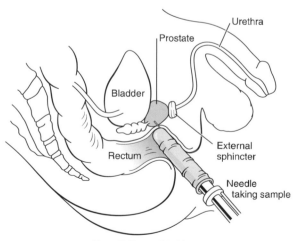

Figure B. The prostate biopsy.

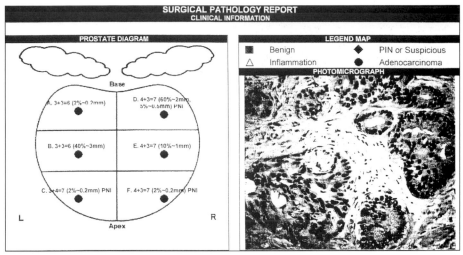

Figure C. 6-core biopsy report.

taken that actually had cancerous cells in it. The amount of cancer in each sample is important; the more cancer, the more the concern. Also keep in mind that the word *impression* is the medical terminology that means the "bottom line" or the "cut to the chase" part of this or most other reports from the doctor.

Other important information from the biopsy can include the words: "High-grade prostatic intraepithelial neoplasia (HGPIN)" or "Atypical Small Acinar Proliferation (ASAP)." These terms do not represent cancer when they are found in a biopsy sample report. Instead, they represent a gray area or "not quite cancer

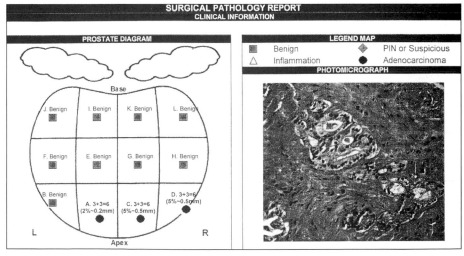

Figure D. 12-core biopsy report.

but not quite normal either." High-grade PIN and/or ASAP are considered pre-cancerous markers and can frequently coexist with cancer or just increase the chance that cancer will be found on a future biopsy. The greater the number of biopsy samples that contain one or both of these markers, the greater the chance of being diagnosed with cancer in the future. The doctor will often recommend a repeat biopsy in 6 to 12 months if a man has one or both of these markers. I tell patients to go over their pathology report carefully with their doctor even if the doctor says there is no cancer. It is important to know if any of the samples contained HGPIN, ASAP, or another marker that lets you know if you should be followed more closely by your doctor.

If you have been diagnosed with cancer, the pathologist looking at your slides will attempt to determine how aggressive your cancer is (called "grading") and if your cancer is contained within the prostate or has spread beyond the prostate (called "staging").

GLEASON SCORES AFTER BEING DIAGNOSED WITH PROSTATE CANCER

The Gleason system is based on how effectively the cells of any particular cancer are able to structure themselves into glands resembling those of the normal prostate. The ability of a tumor to mimic normal gland architecture is called its *differentiation*, and experience has shown that a tumor whose structure is nearly normal (well differentiated) will probably behave relatively close to normal—that is, not very aggressive. To determine a Gleason grade, a pathologist looks at each cancerous tissue sample and assigns it two numbers from 1 (least aggressive) to 5 (most aggressive). Two numbers are given because prostate tumors from a single individual will generally show some variation. In other words, some of the tumor might look aggressive, while some of it may not.

The first number of the Gleason score is the most common or primary predominant type of cancer in the sample and the second number is the second most common tumor type seen on the sample. For example, a 4 + 3 = 7 means a "moderately poorly differentiated" cancer as you can see in the table, but it also means that there existed more of a 4 primary pattern in the sample compared to a 3 secondary pattern. In general, the lower your total Gleason score, the less aggressive the cancer, and the higher the Gleason score the more aggressive the cancer. This also may be true of the individual numbers that make up the total score. A 4 + 3 is slightly more aggressive as compared to a 3 + 4, even though both add up to 7, because the primary or majority predominant tumor type is 4 (more aggressive) in the first case and 3 (less aggressive) in the second case. In addition, it is important that you know that it is very rare today to be diagnosed with a total Gleason score of 2 to 4 or even 5. In fact, the average or common type of prostate cancer diagnosed currently is a total Gleason score of 6 or 7. Why? Many pathologists believe that Gleason scores of 2–5 are not completely or actually cancer in some cases but have a lot of normal features. Therefore, Gleason scores of 6 and 7 now represent the majority of the prostate tumors diagnosed, and Gleason scores of 8 to 10 remain as the group of tumors that are generally more aggressive. A summary of the potential Gleason scores that could appear on your pathology report follows in the table. Keep in mind that every single prostate biopsy sample with cancer will be assigned its own Gleason score, but please discuss what your over-all Gleason score means with your doctor.

Table 1 - Possible Gleason Scores

Gleason Scores	What Does That Tell Us?
1+1, 2+1, 1+2, 1+3 2+1, 2+2 3+1	2–4 = Well differentiated cancer or not aggressive
1+4, 1+5 2+3, 2+4 3+2, 3+3 4+1, 4+2 5+1	5–6 = Moderately differentiated cancer or moderately aggressive
2+5 3+4 4+3 5+2	7 = Moderately poorly differentiated or aggressive
3+5 4+4, 4+5 5+3, 5+4, 5+5	8–10 = Poorly differentiated cancer or very aggressive

THE ABCD & TNM CLINICAL STAGING SYSTEMS

Please discuss with your doctor where your cancer has spread based on this system (Figure E). This is a difficult system to explain in a book and it is really best to have your doctor show you where on this system your cancer is, and what this means to you. Keep in mind that numerous tests and not just the pathology report can be used to determine the specific location of your cancer.

TABLE 2 — The ABCD and New TNM Clinical Staging Systems for Localized Prostate Cancer

ABCD	TNM	What Do the Results Mean?
—	TX	The cancer cannot be staged at this time.
—	TO	There is no evidence of a cancer.
A	T1	A cancer that cannot be felt with a DRE or picked up by an imaging machine (X-ray, CT scan, MRI, etc.) or is found by PSA or another procedure, such as a TURP for BPH. This is "localized or confined prostate cancer."
A1	T1a	A cancer that is found during a procedure such as a TURP (not found by a biopsy). The cancer takes up less than 5% of prostate tissue removed in the procedure.
A2	T1b	A cancer that is found during a procedure such as a TURP. The cancer takes up more than 5% of the prostate tissue removed in the procedure.
B0	T1c	A cancer that cannot be felt with a DRE but it is detected by a biopsy in one or both sides of the prostate, because of an initial high PSA level.
B1 or B2	T2	The cancer is only confined or within the prostate, and/or it has invaded the apex of the prostate (where the urethra leaves the prostate), or it has gone into but not beyond the prostate capsule. This is still called a "localized or confined prostate cancer."
B1	T2a	A cancer that occupies only one side (lobe) of the prostate.
B2	T2b	A cancer that occupies both sides (lobes) of the prostate.

TABLE 3 — The ABCD and New TNM Clinical Staging Systems for Advanced Prostate Cancer

ABCD	TNM	What Do the Results Mean?
C1–C2	T3	The cancer goes through the prostate capsule. This is also called "locally advanced prostate disease."
C1	T3a	A cancer on one or both sides of the prostate that is now growing on the outside and going beyond the prostate. This is also called "unilateral (one side) or bilateral (both sides) extracapsular extension."
C2	T3b	A cancer that has invaded one or both seminal vesicles.
C2	T4	A cancer that has spread to or invaded other nearby structures other than the seminal vesicle(s) such as the: bladder neck, external sphincter, rectum, nearby muscles (also called "levator muscles") and/or the pelvic wall. This is also called a "locally or regionally advanced prostate cancer."
—	NX	The lymph nodes cannot be staged at this time.
—	NO	No lymph nodes near the prostate have cancer (or metastasis). These are also called "regional lymph nodes."
D1	N1	Cancer in a regional node or nodes near the prostate. This is also called a "regionally advanced prostate cancer."

Note: The regional lymph nodes are in the pelvic area and there are 5 sets of them called: Pelvic, Hypogastric, Obturator, Iliac, and Sacral.

ABCD	TNM	What Do the Results Mean?
—	MX	Metastasis or cancer spread far beyond the prostate (also called "distant metastasis") cannot be staged at this time.
—	MO	There is no metastasis or cancer spread far beyond the prostate (also called "no distant metastasis").
D2	M1	Cancer has metastasized or spread far beyond the prostate (also called "distant metastasis"). This is also called "Advanced Prostate Cancer."
D2	M1a	Cancer has metastasized or spread to a node or nodes far beyond the prostate (also called "nonregional lymph node or nodes").
D2	M1b	Cancer has metastasized or spread to the bone or bones.
D2	M1c	Cancer has metastasized or spread to another site or sites in the body far beyond the prostate (such as the liver, lungs, and bones). This is the most advanced category or stage of prostate cancer.

Note: The nonregional lymph nodes are far from the prostate and there are 8 sets of them called: Aortic (also called "para-aortic lumbar"); Common iliac; Inguinal; Superficial inguinal (also called "femoral"); Supraclavicular; Cervical; Scalene; and Retroperitoneal.

Note: M or Metastasis, or cancer spread far beyond the prostate commonly goes to a bone or bones. In addition, during metastasis, the cancer can commonly go to nonregional or distant lymph nodes. Prostate cancer to the lung is uncommon with metastasis but when it occurs it usually is because it has gone along the distant lymph nodes to eventually reach the lung. Liver metastasis or cancer that has spread to the liver is very uncommon and it usually occurs late in the course of this disease.

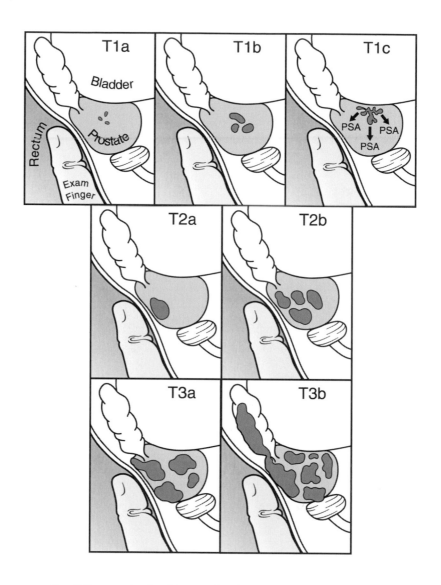

Figure E. The progression of prostate cancer, from the earliest stages to the most advanced, along with the corresponding TNM and ABCD stages.

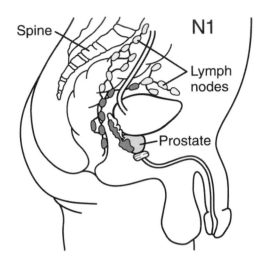

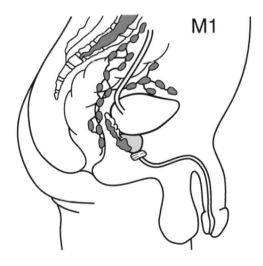

CHAPTER 4

Treatment Options

Once the grade and stage of your prostate cancer are determined, the doctor might summarize your prostate cancer risk category or group as being low, intermediate, or high, which helps to determine the risk of cancer spreading or even returning at some point in the future after treatment. The reason your cancer may be placed in one of these three categories is that it helps you and your doctor decide how aggressive you want to be with your treatment. For example, high-risk patients may receive multiple treatments such as surgery or radiation with androgen deprivation treatment (ADT).

RISK CATEGORY/GROUP	PSA (NG/ML)	GLEASON SCORE	STAGE (LOCATION)
Low (all of the following features)	Less than 10	2–6	Tumor occupies a small area or just one side of the prostate
Intermediate (one or more of the following features)	10–20	7	Tumor occupies a large area of one side of the prostate
High (one or more of the following features)	Greater than 20	8–10	Tumor involves both sides of the prostate

Which type of surgery, radiation treatment, or any other treatment is best when compared to another? This is one of the most common questions I'm asked when it comes to prostate cancer treatment. I often tell patients that "treatment fits personality." This means, since the long-term results are fairly similar between the types of surgery and/or radiation, that a man impacted by prostate cancer should choose which treatment is best for him after an extensive investigation of the options and the slight differences between the options. For example, some patients like the ease of radiation therapy, but others do not like the thought that if cancer should return after radiation then most men cannot have surgery to remove the prostate. Some patients like the fact that surgery removes the whole prostate and the entire tumor, but others do not like the fact that there may be some immediate side effects and recovery time needed. The treatment chosen should fit the patient's personality and situation.

SURGERY

Figures A to C show where incisions are made and what steps are involved in a radical prostatectomy in both the open or traditional surgery and in a laparoscopic or robotic surgery. Figure D shows the reconstruction process following the prostatectomy. The average total time for a radical prostatectomy is 2–3 hours.

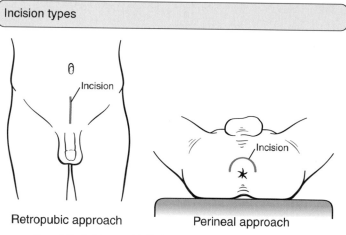

Figure A. The incisions used in the two open types of radical prostatectomy.

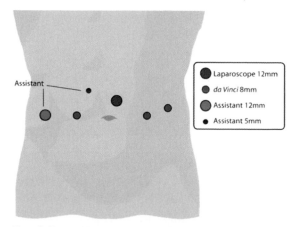

Figure B. The small incisions used in robotic surgery.

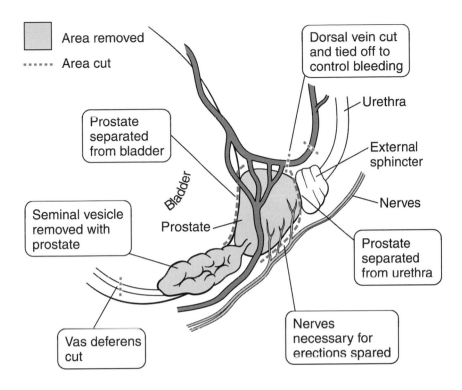

- Area removed
- ----- Area cut

Dorsal vein cut and tied off to control bleeding

Urethra

Prostate separated from bladder

External sphincter

Bladder

Nerves

Seminal vesicle removed with prostate

Prostate

Prostate separated from urethra

Vas deferens cut

Nerves necessary for erections spared

Figure C. The prostatectomy procedure.

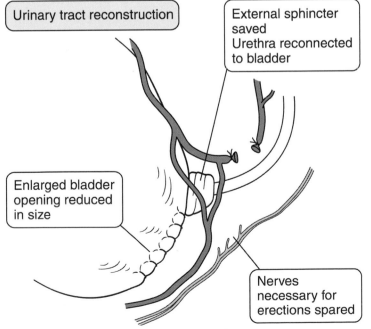

Urinary tract reconstruction

External sphincter saved
Urethra reconnected to bladder

Enlarged bladder opening reduced in size

Nerves necessary for erections spared

Figure D. The reconstruction.

There is little question that robotic surgery has become popular over the past few years. If surgery is your choice, you should review the similarities and differences between the surgery types. Despite the long-term outcomes of the types of surgeries being relatively similar, you should check with the surgeon(s) about the latest differences in the types of surgery in terms of:

- Clinical outcomes such as cancer control
- Erectile dysfunction and incontinence
- Hospital stay and recovery time
- Wound infection and scarring
- Blood loss and transfusions
- Pain

RADIATION THERAPY

In general, radiation is energy that is used in an attempt to destroy prostatic tissue while mostly avoiding injury to nearby organs and tissues. However, the bladder, rectum, and urethra are close to the prostate, so they may receive a small amount of radiation during treatment, which could cause some side effects in the future. Radiation therapy can be used in combination with androgen deprivation therapy (ADT), especially if cancer has spread beyond the prostate or the cancer is aggressive. Radiation therapy usually requires little or no hospital stay, and men can usually continue working and maintain their normal lives during the treatment. Radiation therapy comes in a variety of forms, including different types of external-beam radiation therapy (EBRT) and brachytherapy.

EBRT is delivered from an external source (outside the body). It is usually given in brief sessions (15–30 minutes) by a machine, usually one session each day, 5 days a week, for 5 to 8 weeks. One type of EBRT is known as 3-Dimensional Conformal Radiation Therapy (3D-CRT). A computed tomography (CT scan) is used to create a 3-dimensional picture of the prostate and the surrounding areas so the radiation energy can be given only to the prostate gland. A customized treatment is designed for each patient before the radiation is delivered. Thus, 3D-CRT is an accurate delivery of radiation to the prostate target with the hope of more effective treatment and fewer side effects as compared to standard external-beam radiation therapy.

Intensity Modulated Radiation Therapy (IMRT) is a more sophisticated form of EBRT. Similar to 3D-CRT, a CT scan is used to outline the target and surrounding areas in the patient. The IMRT radiation dose can be changed across the opening of the beam, unlike other EBRTs where the intensity of the radiation beam is fairly constant during the procedure. Tomotherapy is the name of a specialized form of IMRT that allows the beam to hit the target from a variety of directions, and CyberKnife (stereotactic radiosurgery) is another form of EBRT that also allows the tumor to be hit at different angles.

Another type of specialized EBRT that also involves a good deal of pre-radiation target planning is neutron or proton radiation, which uses particles that have different qualities than the photons used in standard radiation. Like other EBRTs, the amount of energy neutrons or protons deliver attempts to maximize the radiation dose that can hit the cancer itself, but at the same time minimizing the amount that hits the healthy tissues. Some men with very aggressive tumors may receive a combination of neutrons or protons with a higher dose of another type of EBRT. There are currently only a few centers in the United States that offer neutrons or protons because it is very expensive technology. Whether or not it really works better than standard EBRT should be a topic of discussion between you and your doctor.

Keep in mind that when a planning CT is used with any type of EBRT, small tattoos are placed on the skin of the patient and the position of the prostate is measured from those markers. However, there are many different techniques used today to better locate the exact position of the prostate before treatment. Some medical centers use ultrasound, others use CT or other imaging techniques, others insert seeds (small markers) into the prostate and take X-rays because the seeds can be seen on an X-ray to help locate the prostate. All of these techniques help to know the precise location of the prostate because the prostate can actually move slightly over time. This ultimately allows the energy to hit the target better and keep it from hitting non-cancerous areas of the body.

Brachytherapy is a type of radiation delivered from inside the body, in which radioactive seeds or pellets are implanted in order to kill the surrounding tissue, including the cancer (Figure E). Before the seeds are implanted in the prostate, a great deal of time is spent understanding exactly where the cancer is and the precise location of the prostate. There are different types of radioactive seeds that may be used, with Palladium 103 and Iodine-125 being the most common. The procedure takes one to several hours.

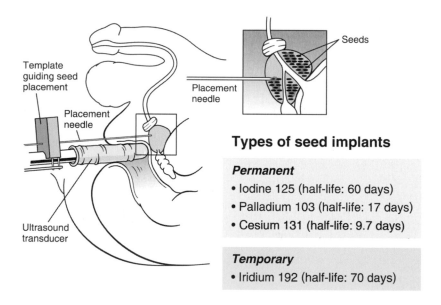

Types of seed implants

Permanent
- Iodine 125 (half-life: 60 days)
- Palladium 103 (half-life: 17 days)
- Cesium 131 (half-life: 9.7 days)

Temporary
- Iridium 192 (half-life: 70 days)

Figure E. A side view of permanent radioactive-seed implantation performed under the guidance of transrectal ultrasound, or TRUS.

Temporary radioactive-seed implantation involves placing an intense radiation source directly in or around the cancer for a short period of time. Done under ultrasound guidance, 12–20 small, flexible plastic needles are inserted through the perineum and into the prostate (Figure F). This procedure requires a short stay in the hospital.

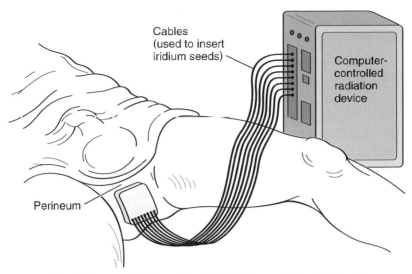

Figure F. Temporary radioactive-seed implantation: Iridium seeds (also called "bars") are inserted and timed using a computer-controlled radiation device.

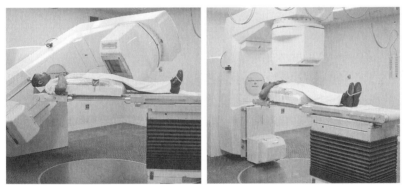

Figure G. External beam radiation therapy.

The most desirable type of radiation for you is simply too important (like all other treatments) to be handled by a book and should always be decided by you and your doctor.

CRYOSURGERY

During cryosurgery (Figure H), several supercooled probes are inserted through the perineum (the area between the anus and scrotum) into different areas of the prostate. A warmer may also be used to reduce side effects. A transrectal ultra-sound probe (covered with a condom) is inserted into the rectum to help guide the procedure. When the probes are removed, each of the punctures requires a single suture, or stitch, to close. Some

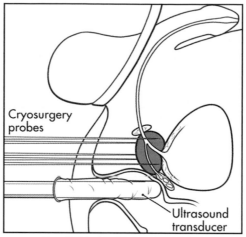
Figure H. Side view of cryosurgery procedure.

doctors are also using cryosurgery today for men with a prostate who have a rising PSA after radiation treatment.

EXPERIMENTAL OPTIONS FOR LOCALIZED PROSTATE CANCER (NON-FDA APPROVED)

Active Surveillance (also known as "watchful waiting")

For a small number of patients, usually older men diagnosed with a non-aggressive prostate tumor that is small in size, an option may be to forego treatment for a period of time and monitor the situation carefully. This means you do not get any treatment for prostate cancer in the short term, but if the cancer shows signs that it is growing and may impact your life, then an effective treatment may be offered. There is no standard protocol for how to handle "active surveillance" patients, but I have summarized the most common procedures or methods used by the doctors who have researched this treatment. An important topic to discuss with your doctor is the most common reason for discontinuing active surveillance thus far from research, which is the anxiety of knowing that you have an untreated cancer. Although the disease may not have progressed, the uncertainty of not being treated when a patient knows that they have cancer may not be acceptable to all patients. This can be too intimidating for some, and not as much of an issue for others.

WHAT GENERAL REQUIREMENTS HELP A MAN QUALIFY FOR ACTIVE SURVEILLANCE?
PSA Level of less than or equal to 10
Gleason score equal to or less than 6
Stage T1c to T2a
Less than 3 biopsy samples with cancer & less than 50% of cancer in any one sample (however, this depends on age and other diseases the patient might have)
Older age

WHAT KIND OF SCHEDULE SHOULD BE GENERALLY FOLLOWED IF YOU ARE ON ACTIVE SURVEILLANCE?
DRE and PSA at least every 3 months initially for at least 2 years, then every 6 months if the PSA becomes stable. PSA, PSA doubling time, PSA density, free to total PSA and/or PSA velocity may all be calculated or determined while on active surveillance.
At least a 10-12 core/sample repeat biopsy after 1 year, and then every 1-3 years after this biopsy.
Some doctors like to use imaging tests every so often, for example, transrectal ultrasound (TRUS), endorectal coil MRI, or another test that takes a picture of the prostate.
If the PSA doubling time is less than 2-3 years (in most cases, this should be based on at least 8 PSA measurements), there should be a discussion of potentially treating your cancer.
If on any biopsy the cancer has progressed to a Gleason 7 (4+3 in general) or higher, there should be a discussion to potentially treat your cancer.
Note: There are several clinical trials right now that take men on active surveillance and treat them minimally with a pill, for example, dutasteride or finasteride or androgen deprivation, but these are all experimental studies with no long-term research.

High-Intensity Focused Ultrasound (HIFU)

This is considered an experimental treatment in the United States and it does not have long-term safety or effectiveness research. HIFU is an ultrasound beam that is focused at a fixed focal point (like a magnifying glass focusing sunlight on an object). It creates high energy that can destroy tissue. This means the temperature can become 80 to 100 degrees Celsius at the focused point, but not necessarily near the area or in the path of the beam. HIFU literally allows for "cooking" certain areas of the prostate from the outside inward. HIFU is a single outpatient procedure that generally uses a spinal anesthetic, and it has also been repeated in some cases if it fails the first time. It is being tested to potentially treat localized prostate cancer, and is also being tested for men who have their cancer return after conventional treatment. It is touted in some cases to have lower rates of incontinence and erectile dysfunction as compared to conventional treatment, but again this cannot be substantiated because there are no long-term data. Patients can usually return to work the next day. Immediately after HIFU, the prostate gland swells, which can cause bladder outlet obstruction and urinary retention. As the swelling decreases after 3–4 weeks, the patient is usually able to urinate and empty his bladder. Therefore, a catheter is required for several weeks after the procedure. This catheter can be placed through the penis or through a small hole in the lower abdomen directly into the bladder (suprapubic catheter). Still, there is a risk of incontinence, erectile dysfunction, risk of holes forming that can connect with different parts of the body (known as a "fistula"), and sloughing of dead tissue in the urine. Larger prostates can be a problem with HIFU because the heat can only go a certain distance in the prostate tissue. Androgen deprivation is used for larger prostates to first shrink the gland.

HIFU was approved by Health Canada as a potential treatment (available since January 2006), and some individuals have traveled there and other places to receive it. However, they have to pay out of pocket for the treatment, which can cost as much as $20–30,000 dollars per session. Regardless, this is an experimental procedure that needs more long-term research.

NEW OPTIONS AND THOUGHTS ABOUT ADVANCED PROSTATE CANCER

A rising PSA without symptoms is becoming the most common indication of advancing cancer. An area that is still being researched is the timing of treatment for advanced prostate cancer. Treat earlier and there are side effects (see chapter 5), but perhaps the disease can be controlled if treatment begins earlier, and other side effects of advanced disease can be prevented? Treat later and there are no immediate side effects, but perhaps the anxiety of waiting to be treated creates a problem? For men with PSA-only disease (no symptoms), the answer is not yet clear but research suggests that for men with more aggressive disease, the earlier the better.

Androgen Deprivation Treatment

One treatment for advanced and locally advanced cancer is androgen deprivation treatment (ADT), also known as LHRH treatment, which stops the production of testosterone by the human body. Many prostate cancer cells need testosterone to grow, so suppressing testosterone can impede the progress of an advancing cancer.

Androgen deprivation treatment (ADT) can be accomplished a number of ways:

- An LHRH injection can be given.
- An LHRH injection can be given along with an anti-androgen pill.
- The testicles can be surgically removed.
- An anti-androgen pill can be taken after the testicles have been removed.
- An anti-androgen pill can be taken.

LHRH injections are administered in the buttocks or abdomen. LHRH injections (for example, Lupron®) can be given every month, every three months, every four months, or even less frequently.

Is it best to give androgen deprivation treatment (ADT) immediately after a diagnosis of advanced or locally advanced prostate cancer, or is it preferable to wait until a man has symptoms? Regardless, some patients and doctors want to start ADT immediately, others favor a high PSA before treating, and others wait until there is clear evidence of advanced cancer from an imaging test, such as a bone scan. Each situation is different and should be discussed with your doctor.

Some research suggests that giving continuous ADT to some patients is ideal, but other research suggests that some men with non-aggressive tumors may do as well with more intermittent (off and on, off and on) ADT (referred to as IADT). In fact, IADT is being compared to continuous ADT in some very large clinical trials around the world right now. Since IADT is considered experimental right now, there are no absolute guidelines, but IADT is usually administered by starting a man on ADT (LHRH injection plus an anti-androgen pill) for about 6–12 months, until the PSA is undetectable. The man is then taken off ADT and his testosterone is allowed to rise. When the PSA starts to rise and reaches a certain point, ADT is restarted and the cycle continues. Again, it is not known if this therapy produces similar, better, or worse results than continuous ADT, but it does seem to improve the quality of life in some areas, such as sexual side effects. Keep in mind that regardless of the type of ADT (continuous or IADT), at least 10–20 percent of men who remain on ADT for at least 1 to 2 years do not experience an increase in testosterone if the LHRH injections are stopped. In other words, the testosterone-making cells in your body stop making testosterone permanently following suppression.

What happens if a man no longer responds to androgen deprivation therapy (ADT)?

A review of all the options at this point is too extensive for any book. However, a quick overview of some options to help in the discussion with your doctor is provided in this section.

If your PSA continues to rise while receiving LHRH injection therapy (or another primary testosterone-lowering option such as surgery), there are several initial options, including adding an anti-androgen pill, or if you were also already on an anti-androgen pill, the doctor may stop it for several weeks and add another anti-androgen pill or simply move to other options, such as secondary hormonal treatment or chemotherapy. However, only chemotherapy is FDA approved. Keep in mind that, in general, the usual standard of care is to keep a man continuously on LHRH therapy during any other treatment from this point forward. There is evidence that there is still some benefit to be derived by staying on the LHRH therapy, including with chemotherapy or any experimental treatments.

Secondary Hormone Therapy Options to Reduce PSA

The table on page 83 shows some of the many options. Each

NAME OF THE SECONDARY HORMONE TREATMENT	WHAT IS IT/ HOW DO YOU TAKE IT?	HOW DOES IT WORK?	SIDE EFFECTS
Aminoglutethimide	Pill	Blocks production of androgens that come from the adrenal gland	Fatigue, rash, dizziness
Anti-androgen Addition (AAA)	Adding a first, second or third type of hormonal therapy pill, such as bicalutamide, flutamide, or nilutamide.	Blocks the cancer cells' ability to use testosterone.	Can affect the liver; breast tenderness or growth; loss of libido; hot flashes; can be expensive
Anti-androgen Withdrawal (AAW)	Stopping the anti-androgen pills, waiting over several weeks or months to see if the PSA drops	Over time, cancer cells begin to rely on the anti-androgen therapy, so removing it may cause a temporary control of cancer and PSA levels	No physical side effects and the response can be short
Corticosteroids	Pill, injection, or intravenous (IV) options	Generally used in combination with chemotherapy to reduce toxicity	Blurred vision, stomach discomfort
Estrogen	Pill, patch, injection, or IV options	Impacts male hormone levels & may directly kill tumor cells	Blood clots, breast growth and/or pain, increased risk of cardiovascular events; inexpensive
Ketoconazole	Pill	Blocks production of androgens that originate from the adrenal glands	Fatigue, abdominal pain, nausea
Abiraterone (in clinical trials only, but looks promising)	Pill	Blocks production of specific metabolites and androgens that originate from the adrenal glands (CYP 17 inhibitor)	Fatigue

option has unique side effects, so talk to your doctor about the advantages and disadvantages.

Chemotherapy
(The Gold Standard Treatment for Hormone-Refractory Prostate Cancer or HRPC)

Taxotere® (also known as "docetaxel") is the first medication ever approved for the extension of life when it comes to HRPC. It is the drug of choice and should always be discussed as an option for all patients who have HRPC. Some doctors are testing the use of this medication earlier in patients without metastatic disease and those who still respond to LHRH therapy. This drug is especially receiving attention in men with very aggressive prostate cancers. Some of the more common side effects of Taxotere® include low blood counts, fatigue, fluid retention, numbness in the arms and legs, and hair loss. However, doctors have many options today to reduce these side effects(see chapter 5).

Other Strategies to Treat Metastases and Life-Threatening Prostate Cancer

There are several other strategies being used to treat metastases or advancing HRPC, including:

- Bone-Strengthening Therapy (bisphosphonates): There is a class of medications known as bisphosphonates that work by blocking the breakdown of bone itself. Zoledronic acid (Zometa®) is an IV drug approved for use in HRPC. It can help to prevent skeletal problems (fractures) that can occur because of cancer or even hormone suppressive medications. There is some research to suggest that it may also slow tumor growth. It does have some side effects that should be discussed with the doctor, including flu-like symptoms, bone and joint pain, and jaw osteonecrosis.
- Radiation (Spot Radiation): This is targeted radiation at the tumor site, and it is usually used for pain management but it may also kill tumor cells. Radiation can damage the bone marrow in the area being treated so this may cause a lower blood count.

- Radiopharmaceuticals: IV drugs with a radioactive element. The radioactivity collects in the tumor and can damage or kill it. This may also cause a lower blood cell count.
- Surgical Intervention: Involves repairing damage done by the tumor.
- Targeted therapies: Drugs that specifically target cancer cells, such as angiogenesis inhibitors, have fewer side effects. Most of them are in clinical trials, but some of them have already been approved for other cancers. They may be available for prostate cancer patients through compassionate use (see below).
- Vaccines: Two interesting vaccines for the treatment (not prevention) of advanced prostate cancer (Provenge® and GVAX®) are in clinical trials right now. Researchers and patients should learn soon whether or not they help. Talk to your doctor about the latest timelines and results.

COMPASSIONATE USE
What every patient with life-threatening cancer should know

As an important piece of general advice, when a drug has not yet been approved for widespread use but looks promising, patients may be able to access it by working through their doctor. Always inquire about the latest medications for compassionate use if you feel you are running out of options.

CHAPTER 5

Preventing or Treating Side Effects

This chapter will quickly review the common and not-so-common side effects from some of the conventional prostate cancer treatments. We'll consider lifestyle changes, dietary supplements, and prescription medications that may help to alleviate or reduce the side effects.

ANEMIA (AND OTHER LOW BLOOD CELL COUNTS)
What is it?

Blood, or more specifically, red blood cells are less able to carry oxygen to supply energy to cells throughout the body due either to a decrease in number of cells or a problem with the cells themselves. In rare cases, the anemia causes symptoms such as fatigue or shortness of breath.

Which prostate cancer treatment(s) are potentially responsible for this side effect?

Anemia usually happens with androgen deprivation therapy (ADT) and it occurs in the first few months of treatment in 90 percent of men. Testosterone is used in producing a hormone that helps maintain a normal red blood cell count, so a large reduction in testosterone is a common cause of this problem in patients having ADT. The type of anemia that usually occurs with ADT is known as a "normochromic normocytic" anemia, which simply means that the body is still producing normal red blood cells, but just not enough of them. Most men do not need treatment for this condition when it is related to ADT treatment, because the reduction in red blood cell count is usually only 10 percent. After several months, it either resolves itself or simply does not cause symptoms. Other types of anemia, such as microcytic anemia that is commonly caused from a dietary iron deficiency or macrocytic anemia that is commonly caused by a vitamin B12 or folic acid deficiency, are both uncommon with prostate cancer treatment. Other blood cells, such as white blood cells and platelets, can be reduced with certain types of medications, including chemotherapy.

Bottom Line: How can it be prevented or treated?

Lifestyle Changes: Weight lifting or resistance exercise can help to reduce the risk of this condition. A study from Australia showed that lifting weights just two to three times a week helps to stimulate red blood cell production in men on ADT. Doctors do not usually want to give testosterone or another medication to improve this condition unless it is really needed.

Dietary Supplements: None recommended

Prescription Medications: Effective prescription medications (recombinant erythropoietin) that will help produce more red blood cells are always available if the anemia is severe. Additionally, a blood transfusion is an option.

BREAST PAIN AND ENLARGEMENT
What is it?

Also known as gynecomastia, nipples of the breast become sensitive and painful and/or the amount of breast tissue in a man increases.

Which prostate cancer treatment(s) are responsible for this side effect?

Anti-androgen treatment (bicalutamide, flutamide, and nilutamide). The greater the dosage, the greater the chance of this side effect occurring during the course of treatment. Estrogen given to men can also cause this problem.

Bottom Line: How can it be prevented or treated?

Lifestyle Changes: None

Dietary Supplements: None

Prescription Medications: There are two effective ways to prevent this from happening. The first is to take a daily anti-estrogen prescription pill, such as tamoxifen or any drug known as an "aromatase inhibitor." These work by blocking the ability of estrogen to stimulate the breast tissue in men. The only problem is that this pill usually has to be taken daily. The other effective preventive method is to receive a small dose of radiation to each breast (known as "prophylactic breast irradiation"). This takes very little time and usually only needs to be done one time. Finally, for men who have already experienced significant breast enlargement, the option of having a specialist remove some of this tissue has been successful.

CHOLESTEROL LEVEL CHANGES
What is it?

When the blood test for total cholesterol, LDL "bad cholesterol," or "triglycerides" increases, or HDL "good cholesterol" decreases.

Which prostate cancer treatment(s) are responsible for this side effect?

Anti-androgen pills (bicalutamide, for example) are responsible for lowering HDL when combined with LHRH treatment. Additionally, LHRH can increase triglycerides in some men. However, LHRH by itself can significantly increase HDL and this may come as a surprise to many health-care professionals and patients, but it has been a consistent finding in clinical trials. This actually makes sense, because high amounts of testosterone can lower HDL. Regardless, whether or not ADT impacts the risk of heart disease is not well known, but it reinforces the recommendation that prostate cancer patients need to know their cholesterol numbers as well as they know their PSA. This just makes sense in light of the fact that cardiovascular disease is the number one cause of death in men.

How can it be prevented or treated?

Lifestyle Changes: There are so many wonderful lifestyle changes that can change your cholesterol in a positive way and these are covered in chapters 1 and 2.

Dietary Supplements: Niacin is an excellent medication to improve HDL numbers in men who have lower numbers, and fish oil can reduce triglycerides in those with abnormally high numbers. However, keep in mind that all medications have some side effects, for example, hot flashes or liver problems with niacin and potentially a blood-thinning effect with high doses of fish oil. Talk to your doctor about the range of options available to improve your cholesterol and lower your heart disease risk.

Prescription Medications: I am a big fan of "statin" or cholesterol-lowering drug treatments in men who cannot control their cholesterol through lifestyle changes. In addition, recent evidence suggests that these medications may reduce the aggressiveness and progression of prostate cancer. Even if they do not, at least they can reduce the risk of the leading cause of death in men.

A final note—blood pressure seems to be minimally impacted by ADT, unless someone gains a lot of weight—then it can go up. There is some concern that hormonal manipulation may also raise blood glucose or sugar levels and create a diabetic-like risk, but it is interesting that a recent study of men taking vitamin D supplements found a reduced risk of being diagnosed with diabetes while on ADT.

COGNITIVE IMPAIRMENT
What is it?

Inability to remember some things and/or a feeling of mental fogginess or slowness.

Which prostate cancer treatment(s) are responsible for this side effect?

Some studies show that ADT or chemotherapy might cause this, but it is rare and other studies have shown no impact with these treatments. Regardless, if there is some concern at all, please talk to your doctor.

How can it be prevented or treated?

Lifestyle Changes: Mental exercises of all types help to keep the brain sharp (use it or lose it theory). Reading, crossword puzzles, card games, and any other activity that requires the brain to exercise itself, so to speak, can help. Aerobic exercise also helps to keep the human blood vessels clean and to allow good blood flow to the brain.

Dietary Supplements: There is some research to suggest that fish oil or omega-3 fatty acids (EPA and DHA) can help reduce the risk of cognitive impairment. There is very little research on the herbal product ginkgo biloba and it could thin your blood too much, so I do not recommend it.

Prescription Medications: There is some new preliminary research to suggest that low doses of estrogen may help prevent or treat this condition. Estrogen can also reduce bone loss in men on ADT, but it may increase the risk of a blood clot.

DEPRESSION & MOOD CHANGES
What is it?

Feeling sad or listless, uninterested in life.

Which prostate cancer treatment(s) are responsible for this side effect?

In my opinion, just being diagnosed with cancer and going through any treatment can be a challenge to an individual physically and mentally. Therefore, it is important to discuss mental health before, during, and especially after prostate cancer treatment of any kind. Whether it is waiting for the next PSA or trying to get in a clinical trial or experiencing a new side effect, cancer can be stressful. Again, I am a big advocate of you and your partner evaluating your mental health during this time and seeking help if it is needed.

How can it be prevented or treated?

Lifestyle Changes: Heart Healthy = Mentally Healthy! Exercise, exercise, exercise! Research continues to show that it may prevent depression and, in those individuals on anti-depressant medication, it may improve the efficacy of the treatment. Weight lifting or resistance exercise also seems to reduce the risk of depression.

Dietary Supplements: There are some dietary supplements that look interesting, such as SAM-e (S-adenosylmethionine) that has been combined with prescription medication in some instances. SAM-e has also demonstrated a pain-relieving benefit in arthritis, but the dosage (500–1,000 mg/day) or whether to even use it should be up to you and a trusted doctor. Omega-3 fatty acids or fish oil pills also have good research in this area. Of the omega-3 fatty acids in fish oil, EPA and DHA have the most evidence and are best when together in the same supplement or if there is more EPA as compared to DHA. Also, compare prices. These supplements can be expensive and most over-the-counter products have large price differences. There is an herbal product known as "St. John's Wort" that is often recommended for depression and it may help. However, I strongly advise prostate cancer patients to stay away from this herbal product because it has been shown to reduce the effectiveness of many medications, including some cancer drugs.

Prescription Medications: A variety of prescription medications is available and effective today. The most common medication classes are known as "SSRIs" and "SNRIs," and some of these same medications have also been shown to reduce hot flashes. Talk to your doctor about the options.

ERECTILE DYSFUNCTION (ED) AND/OR LOSS OF LIBIDO
What is it?

ED is an inability to get or maintain an erection adequate enough for sexual activity or sexual intercourse, while a loss of libido simply means feeling uninterested in sexual activity.

Which prostate cancer treatment(s) are responsible for this side effect?

Most prostate cancer treatments have the ability to cause some degree of ED and/or libido problems. In general, localized prostate cancer treatment (surgery, radiation, cryotherapy) has traditionally been associated with some ED, and ADT or hormone manipulation has been associated with a loss of libido.

How can it be prevented or treated?

ED can take days, weeks, or months after prostate cancer treatment to occur. Some doctors are encouraging patients to use a variety of ED treatment options (pills, pumps, etc.) soon after treatment to help reduce the risk of future ED problems. Talk to your doctor about this aggressive treatment option.

Lifestyle Changes: Heart Healthy = Erection Healthy. Exercise, blood pressure, cholesterol lowering, weight loss … all can help to improve blood flow to the penis.

Dietary Supplements

TYPE OF THERAPY	ADVANTAGES	DISADVANTAGES
Korean red ginseng (2,000-3,000 mg/day) has helped some men with ED L-carnitine (2,000-4,000 mg/day) was combined with Viagra® after surgery in one study & showed some promise. MACA (1,500-3,000 mg/day) is being tested currently to improve libido in LHRH patients.	Cost effective dietary supplements A few small published clinical trials	Minimal research in prostate cancer patients Minimal research on long-term safety (use it at your own risk) Other supplements may be very dangerous, such as L-arginine in high doses may cause cardiovascular problems in some patients from a recent large clinical trial.

Prescription Medications

TYPE OF THERAPY	ADVANTAGES	DISADVANTAGES
Oral medication phosphodiesterase inhibitors (also known as "PDE-5 inhibitors")	Pills taken by mouth. Effective for most men.	Not effective in patients who have had prostatectomy, unless some nerve-sparing approach was used. Side effects include headache, blurry vision, joint or back pain. Should not be used in some patients. 30–60 minutes wait for response Cannot be taken with some medications.

Reference: University of California San Francisco Medical Center, *Managing Impotence—A Patient Guide*, N. Rahman, S. Rosenfeld, T. Lue, and P. Carroll, 2008.

continued next page

TYPE OF THERAPY	ADVANTAGES	DISADVANTAGES
Intra-urethral suppository	Small pellet placed in the urethra without needles. Few systemic side effects. Effective in some men	Can cause penile pain. Requires training. Side effects include (rarely) painful and prolonged erection of more than six hours, fainting, dizziness.
Penile injection	Highly effective. Few systemic side effects. Works in three to five minutes.	Requires injection. Requires office training. Can cause penile pain. Can cause prolonged erection and penile scars or fibrosis.
Vacuum device	Least expensive. No systemic side effects. Effective in most patients. Battery-operated option now available.	Can cause numbness or bruising. Less "natural" erection. Trapped ejaculate. May be awkward to use.
Penile prosthesis	Highly effective. For men who have failed or are not satisfied with medical treatment of impotence.	Small risk of infection. Requires anesthesia and surgery. May require replacement after many years of use.

FATIGUE

What is it?

A feeling of being tired most of the time.

Which prostate cancer treatment(s) are responsible for this side effect?

The most common causes are ADT, other hormonal manipulating drugs like anti-androgens, and chemotherapy. However, radiation therapy has also been associated with some degree of fatigue in some patients.

How can it be prevented or treated?

This side effect is being taken more seriously because it

is becoming one of the most commonly reported problems with many cancer treatments. The good news is that there are now three different, but somewhat complementary, ways to prevent or reduce fatigue.

Lifestyle Changes: The first way is through a common lifestyle change—weight lifting. One of the most famous prostate cancer lifestyle studies ever done found that men on ADT who lifted weights about three times a week had an approximately 50 percent reduction in fatigue as compared to men who did not lift weights! Wow!

Dietary Supplements: Another method to potentially reduce fatigue is through a few dietary supplements. A large Mayo Clinic study recently showed that 1,000–2,000 mg/day of American ginseng (also known as "Panax quinquefolius") worked significantly better than a placebo to reduce fatigue! Also, past studies of L-carnitine (a compound made by every cell of the human body that helps improve energy levels) in similar and even higher doses may have helped. There is also a simple sugar known as "D-ribose" that when added to a beverage (1–2 teaspoons a day) has helped some patients with fatigue.

Prescription Medications: Last, but not least, the research on existing prescription drugs to reduce fatigue is interesting. Stimulant medications such as methylphenidate look promising, as do anemia drugs, if needed. Additionally, there is a medication taken in the morning known as "modafanil" that has provided some help for breast cancer and other cancer patients. Some doctors use it currently for prostate cancer patients with some success. However, more clinical trials are needed. Other stimulant medications with a good safety record are always being researched and may be available right now.

HAIR CHANGES AND/OR DRY SKIN
What is it?

Hair growth on the head (yes, that is right), hair loss on the rest of the body (arms, legs), and skin that feels more rough or dry.

Which prostate cancer treatment(s) are responsible for this side effect?

ADT can cause hair growth on the head or a slowing of hair loss or a reduced risk of premature baldness. This is generally a side effect that does not get many complaints but needs to be explained. Testosterone is needed to express hair loss or baldness, so when testosterone is eliminated or reduced the human body responds by growing hair again (not a lot) or at least not allowing hair loss to occur. However, the situation is different for body hair. Most men in general lose head hair as they get older but gain more body hair, but the opposite occurs with ADT. Chemotherapy causes hair loss in general, especially on the head in some patients, but this side effect is reduced with some of the newer chemotherapy drugs.

Some men complain of dry skin issues when they are given ADT over a long period of time or certain other testosterone-changing medications. This seems to make sense if you think about menopause and women for a moment. When women lose estrogen over several years (menopause), they are more likely to experience dry skin. Men who have ADT experience a male menopause in about one to three months. So, it seems that dry skin can also be an issue that needs to be discussed.

How can it be prevented or treated?

No treatment is typically recommended for hair changes. There is no treatment needed for hair growth on the head and loss of body hair. Most men just want to know why it is happening. In terms of hair loss, there are wigs and medications that can help. However, in many cases it is temporary, so whether or not to treat it should be up to the individual experiencing it.

Lifestyle Changes: There are plenty of inexpensive and simple pieces of advice for preventing and treating dry skin. Dry air, cold air, indoor heating, friction, and even heavy clothing can make your skin dry, itchy, red, and it can crack easily. Long hot showers and baths are not a good idea unless you are with your significant other. Hot water removes the natural oils that the skin produces. ADT or not, as you get older your body produces less and less protective skin oil. Do not use the antibacterial, deodorant, or perfumed soaps, which can cause drying. Use a mild, moisturizing, and scent-free cleanser. Use warm rather than hot water. Keep the bathroom door closed to keep in the humidity, and do not dry your skin aggressively with a towel after the shower or bath because your skin needs to be a little wet when applying moisturizer.

Use moisturizer early and often, and place it throughout the house. A moisturizer right after a shower in the morning is perhaps the best way to protect your skin. Use a product with glycerin, petrolatum (Vasoline®), fatty acids (stearic acid, for example), ceramide, or cholesterol while your skin is still slightly damp. Reapply during the day as needed. If you use a facial moisturizer, as most people should including men, please use a broad-spectrum (UVA and UVB blocker) product with an SPF of at least 15 to 30.

Increase the humidity in your house. You can put a water-filled bowl near a radiator or heating vent, fill the bathtub, or just use a humidifier. Look for a device that has a humidistat, which is a control that automatically shuts off the device when the target humidity is reached.

Do not use an electric blanket unless it is really needed, because they remove moisture from the skin. Wear soft clothes and try to avoid wool and other rough fabrics. Try to wear cotton or silk next to your skin, and use an unscented fabric softener to avoid chemicals and perfumes that can cause excess drying. Use lip moisturizer with an SPF of 15 or more in it, or even petroleum jelly if you need it. You can treat cracked heels with moisturizers with lactic acid or urea and cotton-lined plastic or rubber gloves are a good way to go when cleaning dishes.

Dietary Supplements and *Prescription Medications*: None needed.

HOT FLASHES/HOT FLUSHES
What is it?

Sudden, at times dramatic, feeling of heat; may last seconds or minutes at a time and may occur regularly throughout the day or once in a while.

Which prostate cancer treatment(s) are responsible for this side effect?

Any treatment that reduces male hormone levels (ADT) can cause hot flashes, but the frequency and severity of hot flashes vary dramatically from one individual to another.

How can It be prevented or treated?

If you follow the steps in this section, you will become more familiar with how serious your hot flashes are and whether or not they should be treated by conventional or alternative treatment, or if they should just be left alone. In hot flash clinical trials, most patients responded to some type of minimal intervention, but some patients can experience hot flashes that do not respond to simple lifestyle changes. For most mild to moderate hot flashes, a prescription drug is not needed, but for moderate to severe hot flashes, a prescription drug is usually needed. In the past, most men received prescription medical treatment for hot flashes. Researchers have learned from studies of women going through menopause that lifestyle changes may play a large role in the management of hot flashes. Before deciding with your doctor about the proper treatment for your hot flashes, you need to determine the frequency and severity of the hot flashes.

SEVERITY	SCORE	LENGTH/ DURATION	OBSERVATIONS
MILD Hot Flash	1 point	Less than 1 minute	Warm & slightly uncomfortable, no perspiration
MODERATE Hot Flash	2 points	Less than 5 minutes	Warmth involving more of the body, perspiration, taking off some layers of clothing
SEVERE Hot Flash	3 points	Greater than 5 minutes	Burning warmth, disruption of normal life activities such as sleep or work, excessive perspiration, frequent thermostat changes in your house
VERY SEVERE Hot Flash	4 points	Time is not an issue	Complete disruption of normal activities to the point where it would make you consider discontinuing the androgen-deprivation treatment

PERSONAL HOT FLASH DIARY

Name _____

Week Starting _____

	Hot flashes per day				Points				Total number of flashes	Total points
	Mild	Moderate	Severe	Very Severe	Mild (1 pt each)	Moderate (2 pts each)	Severe (3 pts each)	Very Severe (4 pts each)		
Mon										
Tue										
Wed										
Thu										
Fri										
Sat										
Sun										
					Summary for the Week					

Weekly Average Hot Flash Intensity Score: _____

(Divide weekly points by total number of hot flashes)

Other Observations: _____

_____

_____

_____

_____

_____

_____

_____

_____

_____

_____

HOT FLASH TREATMENTS	% REDUCTION	ADVANTAGES & DISADVANTAGES
Lifestyle Changes • Low-impact exercise • Stress reduction • Controlled breathing • Avoid hot beverages • Use ice cubes/cool beverages/fans • Wear loose-fitting clothing • Reduce room temperature	25–50%	• My first choice along with alternative medicines for most men because using a hot flash diary and these options are effective enough for the majority of men. • Low cost • Does not work for severe hot flashes & prescription medications should be used in these cases.
Alternative Treatments • Acupuncture (1 to 2 times a week) • Black cohosh pills (1–2 pills a day) • Flaxseed powder (2–3 tablespoons per day) • Red clover pills (1–2 pills a day) • Sesame seed powder (2–3 tablespoons a day) • Soy protein powder (several servings a day)	25–50%	• My first choice along with lifestyle changes • Low cost • Does not work for severe hot flashes & prescription medications should be used in these cases. • Discuss supplements with your doctor before starting any treatments to be sure that they will not interfere with your cancer therapy.
Placebo/Clonidine	25–40% (WOW!)	Cheap!
Gabapentin	50–60%	• A range of doses, simple to take, but has numerous potential side effects.
SSRIs & SNRIs fluoxetine paroxetine sertraline venlafaxine	50–60%	• Many options and doses, but has gastrointestinal side effects.

INCONTINENCE/LOSS OF URINARY CONTROL
What is it?

This is a partial or complete loss of urinary control, which is also known as leakage and dribbling.

Which prostate cancer treatment(s) are responsible for this side effect?

Treatments for prostate cancer such as surgery, radiation, and cryosurgery are the more common causes, but this side effect has been reduced dramatically over the years. Today, only a small percentage of patients experience incontinence that requires a pad after treatment.

How can it be prevented or treated?

The prevention and treatment of incontinence is a large field of medicine and is beyond the scope of this book. There are many options available for prevention and treatment, including Kegel exercises (also called special perineal exercises) that can be done before and after treatment. These exercises involve strengthening the pelvic muscles by deliberately stopping and starting the urine flow. When not urinating, the same results can be achieved by tightening the muscles of the pelvis or buttocks. Regular practice of the Kegel exercises (talk to your doctor about how often) may reduce leakage or correct it permanently according to some doctors, but the results may vary from individual to individual. On average these exercises are repeated at least several times a day for several weeks or months. The opinions of doctors on the importance of these exercises and on other incontinence treatments after prostate treatment can vary significantly. Keep in mind that special undergarments, briefs, pads, pills, inserts (catheter), injections, biofeedback, and even surgery are all viable treatment options for mild to severe incontinence.

MUSCLE WEAKNESS/ATROPHY AND MUSCULOSKELETAL PAIN
What is it?

Loss of muscle/strength (also known as "sarcopenia") and/or pain in the muscle and/or joints.

Which prostate cancer treatment(s) are responsible for this side effect?

Any treatment that impacts or simply reduces male hormone levels (ADT) may cause muscle changes.

How can it be prevented or treated?

Lifestyle Changes: No surprise here! Weight lifting or resistance exercise and regular aerobic exercise of any type are the best ways to reduce the risk of muscle loss and weakness. Higher protein intakes may help, but talk to the nutritionist about how much you really need because extremely high protein intakes can cause abnormal changes in your kidneys, especially if you already have kidney issues.

Dietary Supplements: Recent research suggests that most men on ADT do not get the recommended daily intake of calcium, which is 1,200 to 1,500 mg per day. That, along with vitamin D, may help this problem. Only 1 to 2 pills of calcium carbonate per day are enough to meet your daily intake (see chapter 2). Recent research with vitamin D suggests that supplementation with an average of 800–1,000 IU may help reduce muscle atrophy and/or pain, but ideally it would be best to first get a vitamin D blood test (25-OH vitamin D test) before deciding with your doctor if you need more or less. A common dietary supplement that is used to improve muscle size and strength is creatine monohydrate powder, but the research is preliminary on this product. Most studies only use 5 grams or a teaspoon a day in a beverage for men who lift weights on a regular basis. As always, talk to your doctor about the latest research.

Prescription Medications: Some men inquire about growth hormone (GH) or other anabolic steroids to improve muscle mass, but there is a concern about long-term safety, cost, and the potentially lower quality of the muscle increase, despite a potential quantity increase. Talk to your doctor about these latest treatments. Over-the-counter pain medications can reduce muscle and joint pain discomfort when taken on a regular basis. Rarely, some men have had generalized body aches and pain (some call it "androgen deprivation syndrome") and some doctors have been able to control this problem with the use of low-dose prescription steroid medications.

OSTEOPOROSIS/BONE LOSS
What is it?

Osteoporosis is a weakening of your bones that can lead to an increased risk of bone fracture.

There are no symptoms until a bone fracture occurs, so we need to consider how to prevent this from happening. First, we will discuss how bone loss is diagnosed. And then we will discuss how to prevent bone loss through lifestyle changes and what role calcium and vitamin D have in bone health.

An imaging (picture) test is used to help determine the status of your bone health. An imaging test usually takes a picture of one or several sites of the body and then your bones are compared to those of a 25- to 30-year-old male, the benchmark age range where individuals have the optimal bone health. If your bone or bones are similar to the benchmark, then this is considered normal. If your bones are a little less dense or a little weaker than the benchmark, this is called osteopenia. Osteoporosis is when your bones are much weaker than the benchmark. Finally, if you have already had a fracture and your bones are much weaker than a young person's, then this is called severe osteoporosis. The weaker your bones are compared to a young person's, and the more bone loss you have experienced, the more likely that you will experience a fracture in the future unless intervention occurs that reduces your risk of continued bone loss.

There are several devices available today to help your doctor determine the relative state of your bones. The three most common are compared below.

TESTS	ADVANTAGES	LIMITATIONS
Dual-Energy X-ray Absorptiometry (DEXA)	Fairly inexpensive. Low radiation exposure. Rapid and easy to perform. Most multiple site-specific test for spine, hip, wrist. Recommended for most men.	Osteoarthritis of the lumbar spine and/or aortic calcifications falsely elevate measurement in older patients.
Heel Ultrasound (HUS)	Cheap, rapid, easy to perform in office setting. Low risk to patient. May assess initial risk for fracture.	Lacks overall sensitivity. Little known about accuracy of measurements over time. Not recommended for most men.
Quantitative Computerized Tomography (QCT)	Most sensitive method to detect osteoporosis of the spine. Recommended for some men when DEXA is not adequate.	Expensive. High-dose radiation exposure for patient.

I would make several general recommendations for your consideration when having a bone density screening done:

Recommendation 1: If possible, always have your imaging tests done at the same location, with the same machine, and same health-care professional to reduce error.

Recommendation 2: Always ask the health-care professional at the test site if the device is comparing your bones to those of a man or a woman. Ideally, you want them compared to those of a man.

Recommendation 3: Always ask for a copy of your results from the imaging tests and for a copy of the recommendations as a result of your test. Keep in mind that some individuals may get a test result that says that they have bones that are normal, osteopenic, and osteoporotic all at the same time because the multiple bones tested (hip, spine, and wrist) may be in differing conditions.

Recommendation 4: Make sure you understand the out-of-pocket and insurance-covered costs of the tests.

Recommendation 5: After you get your bone mineral density or osteoporosis test completed, use the web site http://www.shef.ac.uk/FRAX/ from the World Health Organization (WHO) to get another idea of your risk of bone fracture. You will need what is known as your hip (or femoral neck) "T-score" from your test results to complete the questionnaire on the site.

Which prostate cancer treatment(s) are responsible for this side effect?

Any treatment that impacts or simply reduces male hormone levels (ADT) may cause bone loss or weakness.

How can it be prevented or treated?

Lifestyle Changes: No surprises! Weight lifting or resistance exercise and regular aerobic exercise of any type are the best ways to reduce the risk of bone loss and weakness.

Dietary Supplements: Recent research suggests that most men on ADT do not get the recommended daily intake of calcium, which is 1,200 to 1,500 mg per day, and along with vitamin D may help this problem. Only 1 to 2 pills of a calcium supplement per day should be enough to meet your daily intake (see chapter 2 for more information on bone loss). Recent research with vitamin D suggests that supplementation with an average of 800–1,000 IU may help reduce bone loss, but ideally it would be best to first get a vitamin D blood test (25-OH vitamin D test) before deciding with your doctor if you need more or less.

Prescription Medications: The most commonly utilized pills or IV medications to prevent bone loss in prostate cancer patients are a class of drugs known as "bisphosphonates," such as alendronate, ibandronate, and pamidronate, and the most commonly used medication is an IV drug Zoledronic acid (Zometa®). These pills can be taken once a week, or in some cases once a month. Other options include prescription vitamin D injections and pills (cholecalciferol or calcitriol), which have to be taken regularly in the case of calcitriol. Research also suggests that a class of drugs known as selective estrogen receptor modulators (SERMs) may prevent bone loss, and the most commonly used drugs are raloxifene and toremifene, which are both in clinical trials for men and have to be taken daily. Talk to your doctor about potential side effects of these medications.

PENIS/SCROTUM SHRINKAGE (ATROPHY OR GENITAL ATROPHY)
What is it?

There are nerve bundles that run along the prostate and help to control erections. If any of them are injured or become less active, there is less of a stimulus or connection that goes to the penis and scrotum. This can result in a small change in length and/or width of the penis. Additionally, male hormone helps maintain the size of the genital area so when testosterone is reduced this can also potentially reduce the penis and scrotum area.

Which prostate cancer treatment(s) are responsible for this side effect?

Any treatment that may impact the nerves near the prostate and/or male hormone levels could potentially slightly impact penis size. Therefore, most prostate cancer treatments, from surgery to radiation to ADT, could potentially have this impact. Talk to your doctor about it and how it can be prevented.

How can it be prevented or treated?

Prescription Medications: The use it or lose it phenomenon of the human body can help prevent this problem. This means talking to your doctor about regularly using any of the erectile dysfunction treatment methods discussed earlier in this chapter in order to continue to maintain nerve stimulation and the length and width of the penis. Men have used pills, injections, pumps, and other methods to not only improve erectile function but to make sure that there is no reduction in size of the genital area. When the nerves have to be eliminated because of the cancer, talk to your doctor about what you can do about this condition.

WEIGHT GAIN, BELLY FAT/WAIST SIZE INCREASE
What is it?

Gain of non-muscle, fat and weight, especially in the belly or waist area.

Which prostate cancer treatment(s) are responsible for this side effect?

The most common causes are ADT and other hormonal manipulating drugs like anti-androgens.

How can it be prevented or treated?

Testosterone in men is needed to help keep metabolism moving, so anything that reduces testosterone or impacts testosterone can increase the risk for weight gain, especially in the area of the belly. And, as men gain weight, more triglycerides are stored in the belly area and the triglyceride part of the cholesterol test may increase.

Lifestyle Changes: Heart Healthy = Healthy Weight (see chapter 1). The best way to prevent weight gain is to reduce your total caloric intake and to exercise most days of the week for 30 to 60 minutes. This should be done before ADT begins ideally, because once a man gains a few inches or centimeters of belly fat it becomes even more difficult to get rid of it. Other studies of regular weight lifting have found that as a person increases their muscle mass their metabolic rate also increases. Therefore, regular aerobic exercise and weight lifting both help to keep fat off the belly. I like to know a man's waist circumference and pants size before beginning on ADT, so that a goal can be set to maintain those measurements throughout treatment.

Dietary Supplements: The only dietary supplement that has helped improve weight loss when used with exercise recently was fish oil. A study from Australia showed that fish oil (EPA and DHA) at 1 to 2 grams per day could help to reduce an additional several pounds or kilograms! Not dramatic, but not bad. Perhaps by reducing inflammation and triglycerides it may help to reduce weight, but taking too much fish oil can cause weight gain, so be careful. Other dietary supplements that help with weight loss have been a disappointment because they contain too many stimulants (caffeine) or other compounds that are heart unhealthy.

Prescription/Over the Counter Medications/Procedures: A recent study found that statin or cholesterol-lowering medication could reduce weight gain in men on ADT. There are several prescription medications that may help if needed, such as sibutramine (also known as "Meridia®" in the United States or "Reductil®" in many other countries) and orlistat. However, I am not as big an advocate of orlistat because it blocks the absorption of fat. It can cause some interesting side effect issues and is expensive. The best advice I can give you is that, regardless of what is offered to you for weight loss, a dietary supplement or older or newer prescription drug, always make sure that it is heart healthy and brain healthy before taking it. Some of the latest drugs that have run into problems have helped people lose weight but also increased the risk of depression!

Liposuction may reduce belly fat but has only been shown to be cosmetic, which means it has not been associated with heart-healthy changes (lowering of cholesterol, blood pressure). Some men inquire about growth hormone (GH) or other fad anabolic steroids, but there are some safety concerns. Although they may help increase muscle mass and thereby are cosmetically appealing, they are very expensive and have many more side effects as compared to lifestyle changes.

A FINAL NOTE ...

Dealing with a serious illness such as cancer can be very stressful and confusing both for patients and their families. It helps to continue to educate yourself so that your discussions with your doctor are productive and together you develop a treatment plan that best matches your individual needs and situation. No one resource or book can provide all the information on a given topic, but hopefully we've given you an overview with this publication. Remember to make a list of questions before your visits to your health-care provider so that you don't forget to ask certain things that are important to your well being. Work to improve your overall health using the methods described in chapter one. Remember, heart healthy = prostate healthy!

There are a host of resources available to patients and care-givers. I've listed just a few here that may be of particular use. Don't forget, in combating an illness, knowledge can be your best ally!

ADVOCACY AND SUPPORT ORGANIZATIONS

American Cancer Society
www.cancer.org (800)ACS-2345

American Society of Clinical Oncology
www.asco.org

American Urological Association
www.auanet.org

CancerCare
www.cancercare.org (800)813-HOPE

Foundation for Cancer Research and Education
www.cancer-foundation.org (434)974-1303

HRPCa.org.
Developed by and for patients with hormone-refractory prostate cancer; frank, well-researched, patient-centered information
www.hrpca.org

MaleCare
www.malecare.com (212)673-4920

Man to Man, local groups of the American Cancer Society
www.cancer.org (800)ACS-2345

National Alliance of State Prostate Cancer Coalitions
www.naspcc.org (858)459-0631

National Comprehensive Cancer Network
www.nccn.org

National Prostate Cancer Coalition
www.pcacoalition.org (888)245-9455

Patient Advocates for Advanced Cancer Treatments
www.paactusa.org (616)453-1477

Prostate Cancer Education Council
www.pcaw.com (866)477-6788

Prostate Cancer Foundation
www.prostatecancerfoundation.org (800)757-CURE

Prostate Cancer Research and Education Foundation
www.pcref.org (619)461-8181

Prostate Cancer Research Institute
www.prostate-cancer.org Helpline: (800) 641-PCRI

Prostate Forum
www.prostateforum.com

The Prostate Net
www.prostate-online.org (888) 477-6763

Us TOO International Prostate Cancer Education and Support Network
www.ustoo.org Support hotline: (800) 808-7866